مِنهاج العارفين

Minhāj al ʿĀrifīn

Ḥujjatul Islām
Imām al Ghazāli (rh)

Translated by
Alomgir Ali

ISBN: 9798309209446

ACKNOWLEDGEMENTS

I would like to take this moment to express my heartfelt gratitude to my wife, Shahina, and my daughters, Hanifah, Iman, Huda, and Nourah, for their unwavering support and encouragement. I am also deeply thankful to Rachel & Dr Saad for their meticulous proofreading of the translation, as well as to Amna, Taha, and Navin for their steadfast support and invaluable advice. May Allāh ﷾ bless them all abundantly and grant them the best in this life and the Hereafter.

CONTENTS

Translator's Introduction

All praise belongs to Allāh ﷻ, and may salutations and peace be upon our master, the Prophet Muḥammad ﷺ. The subject of spiritual wayfaring (*sulūk*) is of fundamental importance for the growth and development of every believer. It serves as the means through which the heart is purified, enabling one to discern the straight path that leads to Allāh ﷻ.

Allāh ﷻ reminds us in the Qur'ān:

"And do not disgrace me on the Day all will be resurrected, the Day when neither wealth nor children will be of any benefit. Only those who come before Allah with a pure heart ⌜will be saved⌝" (26:87–89).

This journey is not only essential for the average believer but is particularly critical for those who pursue knowledge and scholarship. While the common person struggles with the temptations of material pleasures and the love of wealth, the seeker of knowledge is susceptible to more subtle yet destructive vices, such as self-admiration (*ʿujb*), ostentation (*riyāʾ*), arrogance (*kibr*), contentiousness (*mirāʾ*), sectarianism, and the love of fame and leadership. These inner maladies, often hidden and difficult to detect, can corrupt the soul far more insidiously than the overt challenges faced by many. This is why it is famously said:

"Whoever studies jurisprudence (*fiqh*) but does not embrace the spiritual path (*lam yataṣawwaf*) becomes corrupt, and whoever embraces the spiritual path but does not study jurisprudence falls into heresy. But whoever combines both has attained true realisation."[1]

One of the towering figures of Islamic scholarship who exemplified this synthesis of outward and inward sciences was *Ḥujjah al-Islām* Abū Ḥāmid al Ghazāli. Renowned for his mastery of the intellectual and religious sciences, al Ghazāli came to recognise that the hidden desires and spiritual afflictions of the heart could even corrupt the learned. This realisation led him to pursue a profound integration of the outward sciences with the inner disciplines of the soul.

This brief treatise provides a practical guide to initiating a journey of inner transformation, enabling believers to move beyond superficial acts of servitude to attain the deeper realities of devotion to Allāh ﷻ. It

---

[1] See *Mirqāh al Mafātīḥ*, Mullā Ali al Qāri, 1/335, Dār al Fikr

offers a framework for how to capture the inner realities of worship so that we do not become mere outward practitioners, devoid of the essence of true worship.

We ask Allāh ﷻ to accept this humble effort and make it a means of reward for the author, translator, and readers alike.

Alomgir Ali
Tawfiq Online Learning (www.tawfiqonline.org)
27th Rajab 1446 (27/1/25)
London

Biography of Imām al Ghazāli

Abū Ḥāmid Muḥammad Ibn Muḥammad Ibn Muḥammad al Ṭūsi al Shāfiʿī al Ghazāli (450-505 ah), known as *Ḥujjat al Islām* (the Proof of Islām), was a Persian theologian, jurist, and spiritual master whose profound influence shaped Islamic thought and spirituality. Born in Ṭūs (modern-day Iran), he excelled in Islamic sciences, studying under al Juwayni in Nishapur. At the height of his career, he became the head of the prestigious *Niẓāmiyyah* Madrasah in Baghdad, a leading institution of Islamic learning.

Despite his intellectual success, al Ghazāli underwent a profound spiritual crisis, abandoning his post to seek religious certainty. For nearly a decade, he lived in solitude, immersing himself in spiritual purification and ultimately concluding that true understanding of religion lies in transforming the soul and not merely mastering outward knowledge.

Al Ghazāli's unique contribution was his ability to link outward religious practices to inward spiritual realities. In his magnum opus, *Ihyāʾ ʿUlūm al Dīn* (The Revival of the Religious Sciences), he demonstrated how acts of worship, ethical conduct, and daily rituals serve as vehicles for spiritual refinement and nearness to God. By integrating jurisprudence, theology, and the inward sciences, he bridged the gap between the exoteric (outer) and esoteric (inner) dimensions of Islām. His synthesis of law, theology, and spirituality revitalised Islamic thought, offering a holistic path to both knowledge and seeking proximity to the Divine. Al Ghazāli remains one of Islam's most influential figures, inspiring scholars and seekers across generations.

The text presented here is a translation of a concise treatise attributed to al Ghazāli[2], which offers a lucid and systematic introduction to the spiritual path, guiding the reader—particularly the novice—toward the attainment of gnosis (*maʿrifah*).[3]

[2] For a thorough treatment of the authorship of the text, please refer to the appendix.

[3] Gnosis is a transformative, inner knowledge that transcends ordinary intellectual understanding. It is often experiential and concerns the Divine.

INTRODUCTION

Praise be to Allāh ﷻ who illuminates the hearts of the gnostics with His remembrance and inspires their tongues with gratitude. He grants life to their bodies through their devotion to Him, enabling them to dwell in the gardens of intimacy and ascend to the lofty nests of love. Through His remembrance, they are drawn to Him; through His love for them, they love Him; and through His pleasure with them, they find their ultimate contentment in Him.

Their true wealth lies in their state of neediness, and the harmony of their affairs is rooted in absolute reliance upon Him. He ﷻ has gifted them with the knowledge of the remedies for sins and the cures for hearts. Thus, they become luminous lamps, radiating the light of divine proofs, and holding the keys to the treasures of divine wisdom.

المُقَدِّمَة

الحمدُ للهِ الذي نوَّرَ قلوبَ العارفينَ بذِكرِه، وأنطقَ ألسِنَتَهمْ بشُكرِهِ، وعمَّرَ جوارحَهم بخدمتِهِ، فَهُم في رِياضِ الأُنسِ يَرْتعونَ وإلى أوكارِ المحبَّةِ يأوونَ، ذَكَرُوهُ فذكَرَهُم، وأحَبُّوهُ فأحَبَّهُم، ورَضِيَ عنهم فَرَضُوا عنهُ

رأسَ مالِهمُ الافتِقارُ ونظام أمرهم الاضطرار، علَّمهم دواءَ الذنوبِ، وعرَّفهم طبَّ القلوب، فهم مصابيحُ أنوارِ حجَّته، ومفاتيحُ خزائنِ حكمتِهِ،

Their leader is the resplendent moon, their guide the radiant light—none other than the master of the Arabs and non-Arabs, Muhammad Ibn ʿAbdullāh Ibn ʿAbd al Muṭṭalib ﷺ.

He is the pure fruit, the ultimate realisation of the blessed tree, whose roots are firmly established in monotheism and whose branches reach the heavens, bearing the fruits of piety and righteousness.

"...a blessed olive tree, neither of the east nor the west, whose oil almost gives light even if untouched by fire. Light upon light. Allah guides to His light whom He wills; and Allah presents examples for the people, and Allah is Knowing of all things."[4]

"...And he to whom Allah has not granted light, for him there is no light."[5]

May salutations and blessings perpetually descend upon him. Salutations that ascend to the heavens, illuminating their realms with brilliance, casting their radiant effects upon the gardens of eternity, and bringing solace to the ranks of the Prophets. And may endless salutations and boundless blessings be upon his pure household and his sanctified companions.

---

[4] Sūrah al Nūr: 35

[5] Ibid: 40

إمامُهم القمرُ الطالعُ، وقائدُهم النورُ الساطعُ، سيدُ الموالي والعربِ محمد بن عبد الله بن عبد المطلب، والثمرةُ الزاكيةُ من الشجرةِ المباركةِ التي أصلُها التوحيدُ، وفرعُها التقوى:

{لاَّ شَرْقِيَّةٍ وَلاَ غَرْبِيَّةٍ يَكَادُ زَيْتُهَا يُضِيءُ وَلَوْ لَمْ تَمْسَسْهُ نَارٌ نُّورٌ عَلَى نُورٍ يَهْدِي اللَّهُ لِنُورِهِ مَن يَشَاء وَيَضْرِبُ اللَّهُ الأَمْثَالَ لِلنَّاسِ وَاللَّهُ بِكُلِّ شَيْءٍ عَلِيم} [النور: ٣٥]

{وَمَن لَّمْ يَجْعَلِ اللَّهُ لَهُ نُورًا فَمَا لَهُ مِن نُّور} [النور: ٤٠]

صلى الله عليه وسلم صلاةً تلوحُ في السماواتِ آثارها وتعلو في جنانِ الخلد أنوارها وتطيبُ في مشاهدِ الأنبياءِ أخبارها، وعلى آلهِ الطاهرين وأصحابهِ المطهَّرين.

1
THE GRAMMAR[6] OF THE SEEKERS

The spiritual path revolves around three foundational principles: fear (*khawf*), hope (*rajāʾ*), and love (*ḥubb*).

- Fear is a branch of knowledge (*ʿilm*)
- Hope is a branch of certainty (*yaqīn*)
- Love is a branch of gnosis (*maʿrifah*)

The sign of fear is fleeing, the sign of hope is seeking, and the sign of love is preferring the Beloved over all else.

---

[6] Just as grammar governs the structures and meanings of sentences, the inner workings of the heart are governed by principles of spirituality. See al Qushayri's *Naḥw al Qulūb.*

بابُ البيان نَحو المُريدين

يَدُورُ على ثلاثةِ أُصُولٍ: الخَوفُ والرَّجاءُ والمَحبَّةُ،

- فَالخَوفُ: فَرْعُ العلمِ،
- والرَّجاءُ: فَرْعُ اليَقينِ،
- والمَحبَّةُ: فَرْعُ المعرِفَةِ،

فَدَليلُ الخَوفِ الهَرَبُ، ودَليلُ الرَّجاءِ الطَّلَبُ، ودَليلُ المَحبَّةِ إيثَارُ المُحِبِّ المَحبُوبَ.

The relationship between the sanctuary, the Mosque, and the *Kaʿbah* serves as a profound analogy. Whoever enters the sanctuary of devotional resolve (*irādah*) is safe from creation, whoever enters the mosque is safe from sins, and whoever enters the Kaʿbah is safeguarded from remembering other than Allāh ﷻ.

When the servant awakens in the morning, he contemplates how the darkness of night gracefully yields to the light of day, realising that the emergence of one necessitates the retreat of the other. In this divine interplay lies a profound truth: when the radiant light of gnosis shines upon the heart, it dispels the shadows of sin. If at the time of death his state is one of contentment, he is grateful to Allāh ﷻ for the protection He offered and for his divine accord (*tawfīq*). If, on the other hand, his state is one of displeasure, he then tries to proceed with a firm resolve to strive and reform what he can, realising that there is no refuge from Allah except in Him, and that there is no way to reach Him except by Him. He advances in refining his character, rectifying what he has spoiled of his life, seeking help in Allāh ﷻ to purify his outer state from his sins, his inward state from his defects and severing the ties of heedlessness from his heart. He extinguishes the fire of vain desires, subdues the soul's caprices, and embarks upon the straight path.

ومثالُ ذلك الحَرَمُ والَمسجِدُ والكَعبةُ؛ فمَن دَخَلَ حَرَمَ الإِرادةِ أَمِنَ من الخَلقِ، ومَن دَخَلَ المَسجِدَ أَمِنَتْ جَوارِحُهُ أن يَستَعمِلَها في مَعصيةِ اللهِ تعالى، ومَن دَخَلَ الكَعبةَ أَمِنَ قلبُهُ أن يَشتَغِلَ بِغيرِ ذِكرِ اللهِ عَزَّ وجَلَّ.

فإِذا أصبحَ العَبدُ لزِمَهُ أن يَنظُرَ في ظُلمةِ الليلِ ونورِ النهارِ ويَعلَمَ أنَّ أحدَهُما إذا ظَهَرَ عزَلَ صاحِبهُ عن الولايةِ، فكذلكَ نورُ المعرِفَةِ إذا ظَهَرَ عزَلَ ظُلمةَ المَعاصي عن الجَوارِحِ. فإِن كانت حالَتُهُ حالَةً يَرضاها لحُلولِ الموتِ شَكَرَ اللهَ تعالى على تَوفيقِهِ وعِصمتِهِ، وإِن كانت حالَتُهُ حالَةً يَكرَهُ مَعَها الموتَ انتقَلَ عنها بِصُحبَةِ العَزيمةِ وكَمالِ الجُهدِ، وعَلِمَ أن لا مَلجَأَ من اللهِ إلا إليهِ، كما أن لا وُصولَ إليه إلا بِهِ، فَنَدِمَ على ما أَفسَدَ من عُمرِهِ بِسوءِ اختيارِهِ، واستَعانَ باللهِ على تَطهيرِ ظاهِرِهِ من الذنوبِ وتَصفيةِ باطِنِهِ من العُيوبِ، وقَطَعَ زِنالَ الغَفلَةِ من قَلبِهِ، وأَطفَأَ نارَ الشَّهوَةِ عَنْ نَفسِهِ، واستَقامَ على طَريقِ الحقِّ

Mounting the ship of sincerity, he traverses the seas of divine realities, for the day serves as a guide to the afterlife, the night a guide for the worldly life and sleep as a spectacle of death. He arrives at his final destination in anticipation for what he sent forth and with regret for what has passed.

Allāh ﷻ declares:

"All will then be informed of what they have sent forth and left behind."[7]

[7] Al Qiyāmah: 13

وركِب أَمطِية الصِّدقِ، فإِنَّ النَّهارَ دليلُ الآخرةِ والليلُ دليلُ الدنيا، والنومُ شاهِدُ الموتِ، والعَبدُ قادمٌ على ما أَسلَفَ ونادِمٌ على ما خَلَّفَ. يقولُ اللهُ عَزَّ وجَلَّ:

{يُنَبَّأُ الإِنسَانُ يَوْمَئِذٍ بِمَا قَدَّمَ وَأَخَّرَ} [القيامة:١٣]

2
RULINGS OF THE HEART[8]

The states of the heart are categorised into four types: elevation (*rafʿ*), opening (*fatḥ*), lowering (*khafḍ*), and suspension (*waqf*).[9]

- Elevation of the heart: Occurs through the remembrance of Allāh ﷻ.
- Opening of the heart: Happens through contentment with Allāh ﷻ.
- Lowering of the heart: Is caused by preoccupation with anything other than Allāh ﷻ.
- Suspension of the heart: Is due to heedlessness (*ghaflah*) of Allāh ﷻ.

---

[8] The author continues with the theme of grammar.

[9] All terms correspond to the grammatical states words can be in i.e.

Rafʿ: nominative case

Naṣb: accusative case

Jarr/khafḍ: genitive case

Jazm/Waqf: jussive/ apocopation case

بابُ الأحكامِ

وإعرابُ القلوبِ على أربعةِ أنواعٍ: رفعٌ وفتحٌ وخفضٌ ووقفٌ.

- فرفعُ القلبِ في ذِكرِ اللهِ تعالى،
- وفتحُ القلبِ في الرِّضا عنِ اللهِ تعالى،
- وخفضُ القلبِ في الاشْتغالِ بغيرِ اللهِ تعالى،
- ووقفُ القلبِ في الغفلةِ عنِ اللهِ تعالى.

The signs of elevation are three:

1. The presence of agreement with Allāh's ﷻ will
2. The absence of opposition to it
3. The constant yearning

The signs of opening are three:

1. Trust in Allāh ﷻ
2. Sincerity
3. Certainty

The signs of lowering are three:

1. Self-admiration
2. Showing off
3. Greed by seeking worldly pleasures

The signs of suspension are three:

1. The loss of the sweetness of obedience
2. The lack of tasting the bitterness of sin
3. Over-indulgence in permissible matters

فَعَلامَةُ الرَّفعِ ثلاثةُ أشياءَ:

- وجودُ الموافقةِ،
- وفقدُ المخالفةِ،
- ودوامُ الشوقِ.

وعلامةُ الفتحِ ثلاثةُ أشياءَ:

- التَّوكُّلُ،
- والصِّدقُ،
- واليقينُ.

وعلامةُ الخفضِ ثلاثةُ أشياءَ:

- العُجبُ،
- والرِّياءُ،
- والحِرصُ، وهو مُراعاةُ الدنيا.

وعلامةُ الوقفِ ثلاثةُ أشياءَ:

- زَوالُ حلاوةِ الطاعةِ،
- وعَدَمُ مرارَةِ المعصيةِ،
- والتِباسُ الحلالِ.

3
WATCHFULNESS (*RI ʿĀYAH*)

The Messenger of Allāh ﷺ said:

> *"Seeking knowledge is an obligation upon every Muslim."*[10]

It pertains to the knowledge of the 'breaths' (*anfās*)[11].

The seeker must ensure that their inner self is grateful and humble. If blessings are granted, they should acknowledge them as divine favours. If difficulties arise, they should align their movements and stillness with divine guidance. However, achieving this state requires constant awareness of one's need for Allāh ﷻ in all moments.

---

[10] Ibn Mājah (224)

[11] This refers to the spiritual discipline and awareness of the breaths taken by the seeker (*murīd*) in their journey toward Allāh ﷻ. It is a subtle science emphasising the importance of being mindful of every breath as a gift from Allāh ﷻ, ensuring that it is used in devotion, remembrance (*dhikr*), and seeking closeness to Him.

بابُ الرِّعايةِ

قال رسولُ اللهِ ﷺ : "**طَلَبُ العلمِ فريضةٌ على كُلِّ مُسلِمٍ.**"

وهو عِلمُ الأنفاسِ.

فيَجِبُ أن يكونَ نَفَسُ المُريدِ شُكرًا أو عُذْراً، فإِنْ كانَ قيلَ ففَضل وإنْ رَدَّ فَعدْل فطَائِع الحركةِ بِالتَّوفيق، والسُّكونُ بالعِصمَةِ. ولا يَستَقيمُ ذلكَ لهُ إلا بدَوامِ الافتِقارِ والاضطِرارِ.

The essence of this path lies in the remembrance of death, for reflecting on it brings both relief from worldly burdens and protection from the snares of the enemy (*shayṭān*).

A key to attaining this state is to perceive your lifespan as though it were but a single day. Yet, this requires constant vigilance over time, and the gateway to such vigilance is freeing oneself from worldly distractions (*farāgh*). The root cause of this *farāgh* is the renunciation of the world, and the pillar of renunciation is God-consciousness. The peak of God-consciousness is fear, and its reins are certainty. Certainty is cultivated through seclusion and hunger, strengthened by effort and resilience. Both are guided by truthfulness and the guide of truthfulness is knowledge.

وَمِفتاحُ ذلكَ:

ذِكرُ المَوتِ، لأنَّ فيهِ راحَةً من الحَبسِ، ونجاةً من العَدوِّ، وقَوامُهُ بِردّ العُمرِ إلى يَومٍ واحِدٍ، ولَن يَلتَئِمَ ذلكَ إلا بالتَّفكُّرِ في الأوقاتِ، وبابُ الفِكرِ الفَراغُ، وسَبَبُ الفَراغِ الزُّهدُ، وعِمادُ الزُّهدِ التَّقوَى، وسَنامُ التَّقوَى الخَوفُ، وزِمامُ الخَوفِ اليَقينُ، ونِظامُ اليَقينِ الخَلوةُ والجُوعُ، وتَمامُها الجهدُ والصَّبرُ وطريقُهما الصِّدق، ودَليلُ الصِّدقِ العِلمُ.

4
INTENTION

The servant must infuse every action and every moment of stillness with intention, for as it is said, *"Actions are judged by intentions, and every person will have what he intended,"*[12] and *"The intention of the believer carries greater weight than his deeds."*[13]

A person's intention shift with their circumstances, and thus, the one who concerns himself with his intention will often find himself weary, while most people remain at ease in this regard. For this very reason, there is nothing more arduous for a seeker than the careful stewardship of his intentions.

---

[12] Agreed upon

[13] Al Ṭabarānī: 5942

بابُ النِّيَّةِ

لا بُدَّ للعَبدِ مِنَ النِّيَّةِ في كُلِّ حَرَكَةٍ وسُكُونٍ. «**فإنَّما الأَعْمَالُ بالنِّيَّاتِ وَلِكُلِّ امْرِئٍ مَا نَوَى**». «**ونِيَّةُ المُؤمِنِ خَيْرٌ مِنْ عَمَلِهِ**».

والنِّيَّةُ تَختَلِفُ على حَسَبِ اختِلافِ الأَوقاتِ، وصَاحِبُ النِّيَّةِ نَفسُهُ مِنهُ في تَعَبٍ، والنّاسُ مِنهُ في راحَةٍ وليسَ شَيءٌ على المُريدِ أَصعَبَ مِن حِفظِ النِّيَّةِ.

5
REMEMBRANCE

Let your heart become the *qiblah* of your tongue and allow yourself to be enveloped in the humility of servitude and the awe of Lordship as you engage in remembrance. Know that Allāh ﷻ, perceives the secrets of your heart and observes the outward expressions of your deeds. He hears your whispered prayers and spoken words, so cleanse your heart with sorrow and ignite within it the fire of fear.

When the veils of heedlessness are lifted from your heart, your remembrance of Him will be illuminated by His remembrance of you.

Allāh ﷻ says,

"...And the remembrance of Allah is greater."[14]

This is because He remembers you out of His self-sufficiency and no need for you, while you remember Him out of your utter dependence and need for Him.

---

[14] Al Ankabūt: 45

بابُ الذِّكرِ

اِجعلْ قلبَكَ قِبلةَ لِسانِكَ، واشعُرْ عندَ الذِّكرِ حياءَ العُبُوديةِ وَهيبةَ الرُّبوبيةِ، واعلَمْ أنَّ اللهَ تعالى يعلمُ سرَّ قلبِكَ ويرى ظاهرَ فِعلِكَ ويسمعُ نجوى قولِكَ، فاغسِلْ قلبَكَ بالحُزْنِ وأوقدْ فيه نارَ الخَوفِ، فإذا زالَ حِجابُ الغَفلةِ عن قلبِكَ كانَ ذِكرُكَ به مع ذِكرِهِ لكَ. قالَ اللهُ تعالى: {وَلَذِكْرُ اللَّهِ أَكْبَرُ} [العنكبوت:٤٥]، لأنَّهُ ذِكرُكَ معَ الغِناءِ عنكَ وأنتَ ذَكرتَهُ معَ الفَقرِ إليهِ.

Allāh ﷻ, also says,

"Indeed, in the remembrance of Allāh ﷻ do hearts find rest."[15]

Thus, the heart finds its true peace as well as awe in the remembrance of Allāh ﷻ. Allāh ﷻ says,

"True believers are those whose hearts tremble with awe when God is mentioned..."[16]

Remembrance is of two types:

a. Pure remembrance (*dhikr khāliṣ*): A remembrance that aligns harmoniously with the heart, where nothing is beheld except Allāh ﷻ alone.
b. Unadulterated remembrance (*dhikr ṣāfin*): A remembrance attained by extinguishing one's own preoccupation with the act of remembrance itself, transcending all but the Divine.

As the Messenger of Allah ﷺ said,

"I cannot encompass Your praise; You are as You have praised Yourself."[17]

---

[15] Ra'ad: 28

[16] Al Anfāl: 2

[17] Muslim: 486

فقالَ: **{أَلاَ بِذِكْرِ اللهِ تَطْمَئِنُّ الْقُلُوب}** [الرعد:٢٨]

فيكُون اِطْمِئْنَانُ القلبِ في ذِكرِ اللهِ لهُ ووَجلهُ في ذكرِهِ للهِ. قالَ اللهُ تعالى **{إِنَّمَا الْمُؤْمِنُونَ الَّذِينَ إِذَا ذُكِرَ اللهُ وَجِلَتْ قُلُوبُهُمْ}** [الأنفال:٢]

والذِّكرُ ذِكرانِ:

- ذِكرٌ خالِصٌ بموافقةِ القلبِ في سُقوطِ النَّظَرِ إلى غيرِ اللهِ،
- وذِكرٌ صافٍ بِفَناءِ الهِمَّةِ عن الذِّكرِ. قالَ رسولُ اللهِ ﷺ: **"لا أُحصِي ثناءً عليكَ أنتَ كما أثنيتَ على نَفسِكَ."**

6
GRATITUDE

Every breath a servant takes is a renewed blessing from Allāh ﷻ, deserving of gratitude. The most basic level of thankfulness lies in recognising the blessing as being from Allāh ﷻ, finding contentment in what He has bestowed, and refraining from using His blessings in ways that oppose Him. The highest and most profound form of gratitude, however, is to acknowledge inwardly that all of creation combined is incapable of fully thanking Him for even the smallest of His blessings. This is because the act of expressing gratitude itself is yet another blessing, one that calls for further gratitude, creating an endless cycle of indebtedness to Allāh ﷻ. Thus, the obligation of thankfulness extends infinitely.

If Allāh ﷻ takes charge of His servant, He carries the servant's task of gratitude on his behalf, accepts from him the little he offers, and absolves him of what He knows the servant cannot attain or what weakens him.

"We provide both the former and the latter from the bounty of your Lord. And the bounty of your Lord can never be withheld."[18]

[18] Al Isrāʾ: 20

بابُ الشُّكرِ

وفي كُلِّ نَفَسٍ مِن أنفاسِ العبدِ نِعمةٌ للهِ تَتَجدَّدُ عليهِ يَلزَمُهُ القِيامُ بِشُكرِها. وأدنى الشُّكرِ أن يَرَى النِّعمَةَ مِن اللهِ تعالى ويَرضَى بما أَعطاهُ ولا يُخالِفُهُ بِشَيءٍ مِن نِعَمِهِ. وتمامُ الشُّكرِ في الاعترافِ بلسانِ السرِّ أنَّ الخَلقَ كُلَّهُم يَعجِزونَ عن أداءِ شُكرِهِ على أصغرِ جُزءٍ مِن نِعَمِهِ وإن بَلَغُوا غايَةَ المجْهودِ، لأنَّ التَّوفيقَ للشُّكرِ نعمَةٌ حادثَةٌ يَجبُ الشُّكرُ عليها فَيَلزَمُك على كُلِّ شُكرٍ شُكرٌ إلى ما لا نِهايةَ لهُ.

فإذا تَوَلَّى اللهُ العَبدَ حمِلَ عَنهُ شُكرَهُ فَرضِيَ عَنهُ بِسيرٍ وحَطَّ عَنهُ ما يَعلمُ أَنَّهُ لا يَبلُغُهُ ويُضعِّفُهُ **{وَمَا كَانَ عَطَاءُ رَبِّكَ مَحْظُورًا}** [الإسراء:٢٠]

7
GARMENTS

Garments are a blessing from Allāh ﷻ bestowed upon His servant to cover his body. As Allāh ﷻ says,

"...However, the best clothing is righteousness."[19]

The best garment is that which does not distract your inner state from Allāh ﷻ. When you wear your garment, be mindful of Allāh's ﷻ favour of concealment upon His servants. Therefore, do not expose the faults of others while being aware of your own shortcomings.

Instead, busy yourself with addressing your flaws by continuously seeking refuge in Allāh ﷻ to purify you. If a servant forgets his sins, it is a punishment from Allāh ﷻ and it may increase the servant's insolence to sin even more. Yet had he awakened from the slumber of heedlessness, he would have vividly placed his sins before his eyes, trembling with fear. In the depth of his remorse, he would weep for himself, humbled by the realisation that, despite the veil over his secrets, he stands utterly exposed before his Lord.

---

[19] Al 'A'rāf: 26

بابُ اللِّباسِ

اللِّباسُ نعمَةٌ مِنَ اللهِ على عَبدِهِ يَستُرُ بِهِ البَشَرَةَ، {وَلِبَاسُ التَّقْوَىٰ ذَٰلِكَ خَيْرٌ}[الأعراف:٢٦]، وخيرُ لباسِكَ ما لا يَشغَلُ سِرَّكَ عنِ اللهِ تعالى. فَإِذا لَبِستَ ثَوبَكَ فاذكُر محبَّةَ اللهِ السترَ عَلى عِبادِهِ، فلا تَفضَح أَحَداً مِن خَلقِهِ بِعَيبٍ تَعلَمُهُ منهُ.

واشتَغِل بِعَيبِ نَفسِكَ فاستُرْهُ بدَوامِ الاضطِرارِ إلى اللهِ تعالى في تَطهيرِه. فَإِنَّ العَبدَ إذا نَسِيَ ذَنبَهُ كانَ ذَلِكَ عُقوبَةً لَهُ وازدادَ بِهِ جُرأَةً على المَعاصِي. ولَوِ انتَبَهَ مِن رَقدَةِ الغَفلَةِ لَنَصَبَ ذَنبَهُ بَينَ عَينَي قَلْبِهِ نصاباً، ولَبَكَى عليهِ يَجفُون سِرُّهُ، واستَولى عليهِ الوجلُ فَذابَ حَياءً مِن رَبِّه.

So long as the servant relies upon his own strength and attributes the power of reform to himself, he remains severed from the boundless might and strength of Allāh ﷻ. Therefore, surrender yourself fully to the states of reverent fear and hopeful longing, recognising your utter dependence on Him alone.

"And worship your Lord until certainty (death) comes to you"[20]

---

[20] Al Ḥijr: 99

وما دامَ العَبدُ يَرجعُ إلى حَولِ نَفسِهِ وقُوَّتِها انقَطَعَ عَن حَولِ اللهِ وقُوَّتِهِ، فاطرَحْ همتَكَ بَينَ يدَي الخَوفِ والرَّجاءِ.

{وَاعْبُدْ رَبَّكَ حَتَّى يَأْتِيَكَ الْيَقِين} [الحجر:٩٩]

8
THE NIGHT PRAYER

When you rise from your bed, lift your heart above the bedding of idleness. Awaken yourself from the sleep of ignorance and rise with all of your being to the One who grants you life and returned your soul back to your body. Reflect upon your movements and stillness and ascend with your heart toward the celestial realms, and do not allow your heart to remain tethered to your lower self, for the self pulls toward the earth, while the heart yearns for the heavens.

Embrace the words of Allāh ﷻ,

"...good words rise up to Him and He lifts up the righteous deed..."[21]

---

[21] Fāṭir: 10

بابُ القِيامِ

فَإِذا قُمتَ مِن فِراشِكَ، فأقِم قَلبَكَ عَن فِراشِ البِطالَةِ، وأيقِظ نَفسَكَ عَن نَومِ الجَهالَةِ، وانهَض بِكُلِّكَ إلى مَن أَحياك. وَرُدَّ إِلَيكَ نَفسَكَ، وقُم بِفِكرِكَ عَن حَرَكتِكَ وسُكونِكَ، واصعَد بِقَلبِكَ إِلَى المَلَكُوتِ الأَعلَى، ولا تجعَل قَلبَكَ تَابِعاً لِنَفسِكَ، فإِنَّ النَّفسَ تميلُ إِلَى الأَرضِ، والقَلبَ يميلُ إِلَى السَّماءِ، واستَعمِل قَولَ اللهِ عَزَّ وَجَلَّ:

{إِلَيْهِ يَصْعَدُ الْكَلِمُ الطَّيِّبُ وَالْعَمَلُ الصَّالِحُ يَرْفَعُهُ} [فاطر:١٠]

9
DENTAL HYGIENE

Use the *miswāk*, for it purifies the mouth and earns the pleasure of the Lord. Purify your outer self from the filth of transgressing others and your inner self from the stain of wrongdoing. Cleanse your deeds of the impurities of ostentation and self-admiration and refine your heart to be crystal-clear in its remembrance of Him. Abandon whatever does not benefit you, for it only brings you harm.

بابُ السِّواكِ

واستَعمِل السِّواكَ فإِنَّها مَطْهَرَةٌ لِلفَمِ مَرضاةٌ لِلرَّبِّ، وطَهِّر ظاهِرَكَ وباطِنَكَ عَن دَنَسِ الإِساءَة، وأَخلِص أَعمالَكَ عَن كَدَرِ الرِّياءِ والعُجبِ، وأَجْلِ قلبَكَ بِصَفاءِ ذِكرِهِ، ودَع عَنكَ ما لا يَنفَعُكَ بَل يَضُرُّكَ.

10
NATURE'S CALL

When you relieve yourself to fulfil your natural need, take it as a moment of reflection, for true comfort lies in the removal of impurities. Cleanse yourself and lower the head of arrogance, close the door to pride and open the gate of remorse. Sit upon the mat of repentance and strive to prioritise His commands, avoiding His prohibitions and enduring His decree with patience. Purify your inner self by abandoning anger and lust, and embrace both longing and reverence in your worship, for Allāh ﷻ praised a people who,

"...Indeed, they used to race in doing good, and call upon Us with hope and fear, totally humbling themselves before Us."[22]

---

[22] Al Anbiyā': 90

بابُ التَّبَرُّزِ

وَإذا تَبَرَّزتَ لِقَضاءِ وَطرِكَ فَاعتَبر، فإنَّ الرَّاحَةَ في إزالَةِ النَّجاسَةِ، واستَنجِ، ونَكِّس رَأسَ هَمتِكَ، وأغلق بابَ الكبرِ، وافتَح بابَ النَّدَمِ، واجلِس على بِساطِ النَّدامَةِ، واجتَهِد في إيثارِ أَمرِهِ واجتنابِ نَهيِهِ، والصَّبرِ على حُكمِه، واغسل شَرَّكَ بترْكِ الغَضَبِ والشَّهوَةِ. واستَعمِلِ الرَّغبَةَ والرَّهبةَ، فإنَّ اللّٰهَ تعالى مَدَحَ قوماً فقال:

{إِنَّهُمْ كَانُوا يُسَارِعُونَ فِي الْخَيْرَاتِ وَيَدْعُونَنَا رَغَبًا وَرَهَبًا وَكَانُوا لَنَا خَاشِعِينَ} [الأنبياء:٩٠]

11
PURIFICATION

When you purify yourself, reflect upon the clearness of water and its ability to purify and cleanse, for Allāh ﷾ has made it blessed. He ﷾ says:

"And We send down blessed rain from the sky"[23]

Use this water to cleanse the limbs that Allāh ﷾ has commanded you to purify. Let your inner purity align with the clearness of the water. Wash your heart of turning toward anything other than Allah. Cleanse your hands of extending toward other than Him. Wipe away pride and arrogance from your head. Wash your feet of treading paths that lead to other than Him. Praise Allāh ﷾ for the guidance He has bestowed upon you regarding His religion.

---

[23] Qāf: 9

بابُ الطَّهارَةِ

وَإِذا تَطَهَّرتَ فَفَكِّر في صَفاءِ الماءِ ورِقَّتِهِ وتَطهِيرِهِ وتَنظِيفِهِ، فَإِنَّ اللهَ تَعالى جَعَلَهُ مُباركًا فَقالَ:

{وَنَزَّلْنَا مِنَ السَّمَاء مَاء مُّبَارَكًا فَأَنبَتْنَا بِهِ جَنَّاتٍ وَحَبَّ الْحَصِيدِ}[ق: ٩]

فَاستَعمِلهُ في الأَعضاءِ الَّتي فَرَضَ اللهُ عَلَيكَ تَطهِيرَها، وَلْتَكُنْ صَفوَتُكَ مَعَ اللهِ كَصَفوَةِ الماءِ، فاغسِلْ وَجهَ قَلبِكَ عَنِ النَّظرِ إِلى غَيرِ اللهِ، واغسِلْ يَدَيكَ عَنِ الامتِدادِ إِلى غَيرِهِ، وامسَحْ رَأسَكَ عَنِ الافتِخارِ بِنغَيْرِهِ، واغسِلْ رِجلَيكَ عَنِ السَّعيِ لِغَيرِهِ، واحْمَدِ اللهَ على ما أَلهَمَكَ مِن دِينِهِ.

12
LEAVING HOME

When you leave your home heading to the mosque, know that Allāh ﷻ has rights over you that must be fulfilled. Among them are serenity and dignity, taking heed from the creation of Allāh ﷻ, whether from the righteous or the impious. Allāh ﷻ, says:

"These are the parables We set forth for humanity, but none will understand them except the people of knowledge."[24]

Lower your gaze from glances of heedlessness and lustful desires. Spread peace, whether by initiating it or by responding to it. Support those who seek assistance in truth and justice. Command what is good, forbid what is evil and guide the misguided if you are among those blessed with wisdom and insight.

---

[24] Al Ankabūt: 43

بابُ الخُرُوجِ

فَإِذا خَرَجتَ مِن مَنزِلِكَ إِلَى مَسجِدِكَ، فَاعلَم أَنَّ للهِ تَعالى حَقوقًا عَلَيكَ يَلْزَمُكَ أَداؤُها. مِن ذلك: السَّكينَةُ والوَقارُ والاعتِبارُ بِخَلقِ اللهِ بَرِّهِم وفَاجِرِهِم. قَالَ اللهُ تَعالى:

{وَتِلْكَ الأَمْثَالُ نَضْرِبُهَا لِلنَّاسِ وَمَا يَعْقِلُهَا إِلاَّ الْعَالِمُونَ}

[العنكبوت:٤٣]

وَغُضَّ بَصَرَكَ عَن نَظَرِ الغَفلَةِ والشَّهوَةِ، وأَفشِ السَّلامَ مُبتَدِئاً ومُجيباً، وأَعِنْ مَن استَعَانَك عَلَى الحَقِّ، وَأْمُرْ بِالمَعروفِ وَانهَ عَنِ المُنكَرِ إِن كُنتَ مِن أَهلِهِ، وأَرشِدِ الضَّالَّ.

13
ENTERING THE MOSQUE

When you stand at the threshold of the mosque, remember that you are about to enter the court of a glorious King whose majesty is beyond compare. He accepts only what is pure, and none may ascend to Him except through sincere devotion. Reflect upon who you are, to whom you belong, and where you have arrived. Consider from which record your name shall be called.

If you have made yourself ready for His service, then proceed with permission and in safety. Otherwise, pause and remain outside like one who finds himself destitute, deprived of means, and adrift from the path of guidance. Yet, if Allāh ﷻ beholds true sincerity in your heart, He will grant you leave to draw near where you shall be wholly consumed in His presence. Allāh ﷻ, in His infinite mercy, embraces His servants with compassion, honours His guests, provides for those who ask, and pardons those who falter. What, then, must be the bounty He bestows upon those who turn wholeheartedly to Him?

بابُ دُخُولِ المَسجِدِ

فَإِذا بَلَغتَ بابَ المَسجِدِ فَاعلَم أَنَّكَ قَصَدتَ بَيتَ مَلكٍ عَظيمٍ قَدره، لا يَقبَلُ إِلا الطَّاهِرَ، وَلا يَصعَدُ إِلَيهِ إِلا الخالِصُ. فَفَكِّر في نَفسِكَ: مَن أَنتَ، وَلِمَنْ أَنتَ، وأَينَ أَنتَ، وَمِن أَيِّ دِيوانٍ يَخرُجُ اسمُكَ؟

فَإِذا استَصلَحتَ نَفسَكَ لِخِدمَتِه، فَادخُل فَلكَ الإِذنُ وَالأَمانُ، وَإِلَّا فَقِف وَقُوفَ مُضطَرٍّ قَد انقَطَعَت عَنهُ الحِيَلُ وَانسَدَّت عَنهُ السُّبُلُ. فَإِذا عَلِمَ اللّٰهُ مِن قَلبِكَ الإِلتِجاءَ إِلَيه، لَكَ فَتَكونُ أَنتَ بِلا أَنتَ. وَاللّٰهُ يَرحَمُ عَبدَهُ وَيُكرِمُ ضَيفَهُ وَيُعطِي سَائِلَهُ وَيَبرُّ المعْرِضَ عَنهُ، فَكَيفَ المُقبِلُ إِلَيه؟

14
OPENING THE PRAYER

When you turn your face toward the *qiblah*, direct your heart too toward the Truth (Allāh). Do not approach the prayer in a relaxed state for you are not from the people of spiritual expansion (*inbisāṭ*). Recall that you will stand before the Greatest Sovereign, the King of Kings, on the Day of the Greatest Assembly. Stand with your feet firmly grounded in fear and hope and lift your heart above worldly distractions and creations. Direct your supplication to Him, for He does not turn away a pleading servant nor ignore the call of a sincere seeker.

When you declare, "Allāh is the Greatest," then know with certainty that nothing is greater than Him, nor does He require your service or remembrance. This is because neediness is a mark of the impoverished, which in turn is a sign of createdness. Whereas self-sufficiency is from the attributes of His essence.

بَابُ افْتِتَاحِ الصَّلَوَاتِ

فَإِذَا اسْتَقْبَلْتَ بِوَجْهِكَ الْقِبْلَةَ، اسْتَقْبِلْ بِقَلْبِكَ الحَقَّ، وَلا تَنْبَسِطْ فَلَسْتَ مِنْ أَهْلِ الانْبِسَاطِ، وَاذْكُرْ وُقُوفَكَ بَينَ يَدَيْهِ يَوْمَ الْعَرْضِ الأَكْبَرِ، وَقِفْ عَلَى قَدَمَيْ الخَوْفِ وَالرَّجَاءِ، وَارْفَعْ قَلْبَكَ عَنِ النَّظَرِ إِلَى الدُّنْيَا وَالخَلْقِ، وَأَرْسِلْ هِمَتَكَ إِلَيْهِ؛ فَإِنَّهُ لا يَرُدُّ الآبِقَ وَلا يَخِيبُ السَّائِلِ.

فَإِذَا قُلْتَ: «اللّٰهُ أَكْبَرُ»، فَاعْلَمْ أَنَّهُ لا يَحْتَاجُ إِلَى خِدْمَتِكَ لَه ذِكْرِكَ إِيَّاهُ، لأَنَّ الحَاجَةَ مِنْ جُمْلَةِ الْفُقَرَاءِ، وَذَلِكَ سِمَةُ الخَلْقِ، وَالْغِنَى مِنْ صِفَاتِ ذَاتِه.

He ﷻ has decreed upon His servants the acts of worship as a means to draw them nearer to His boundless forgiveness, to envelop them in His infinite grace and abundant rewards, and to safeguard them from His displeasure and punishment.

Allāh ﷻ, says:

"...and (He) bound them to the spirit of God-consciousness: for they were most worthy of this [divine gift], and deserved it well."[25]

In another verse He ﷻ says:

"But as it is, God has caused [your] faith to be dear to you, and has given it beauty in your hearts"[26]

Thus, be grateful to Him ﷻ since He granted you the honour of standing before Him for:

"He is the Lord who should be heeded, the Lord of forgiveness."[27]

---

[25] Al Fatḥ: 26

[26] Al Ḥujurāt: 7

[27] Al Muddaththir: 56

وَإِنَّمَا وَظّفَ عَلَى عَبِيدِهِ وَظَائِفَ لِيُقَرِّبَهُمْ بِهَا إِلَى عَفْوِهِ وَرَحْمَتِهِ، وَيُبْعِدَهُمْ بِهَا مِنْ سَخَطِهِ وَعُقُوبَتِهِ. قال اللّٰهُ عز وجلّ: {**وَأَلْزَمَهُمْ كَلِمَةَ التَّقْوَى وَكَانُوا أَحَقَّ بِهَا وَأَهْلَهَا وَكَانَ اللَّهُ بِكُلِّ شَىْءٍ عَلِيمًا**} [**الفتح:٢٦**] وقال عزَّ من كان قائل: {**وَلَٰكِنَّ اللَّهَ حَبَّبَ إِلَيْكُمُ الإِيمَانَ وَزَيَّنَهُ فِي قُلُوبِكُمْ**} [**الحجرات:٧**] الآية. واشْكُرْ اللّٰهَ إِذْ جَعَلَكَ أهلاً للوُقوفِ بين يَدَيْهِ فَإِنّهُ {**أَهْلُ التَّقْوَى وَأَهْلُ الْمَغْفِرَةِ**} [**المدثر:٥٦**]

15
RECITATION

Allāh ﷻ says,

"When you recite the Quran, seek God's protection from the outcast, Satan. He has no power over those who believe and trust in their Lord. His power is only over those who ally themselves with him..."[28]

"It has been decreed for such devils that whoever takes them as a guide will be misguided..."[29]

When you recite, remember the covenant of Allāh ﷻ upon you in His revelation. Observe how you read His words and reflect on their meanings. Stand in awe at His promises and threats, and ponder His parables, advice, commands, prohibitions, and unequivocal and equivocal verses.

[28] Al Naḥl: 98-100

[29] Al Ḥajj: 4

بَابُ القِرَاءَةِ

قَالَ اللَّهُ تَعَالَى:

﴿فَإِذَا قَرَأْتَ الْقُرْآنَ فَاسْتَعِذْ بِاللَّهِ مِنَ الشَّيْطَانِ الرَّجِيمِ﴾

[النحل: ٩٨].

﴿إِنَّهُ لَيْسَ لَهُ سُلْطَانٌ عَلَى الَّذِينَ آمَنُوا وَعَلَى رَبِّهِمْ يَتَوَكَّلُونَ﴾

[النحل: ٩٩].

﴿إِنَّمَا سُلْطَانُهُ عَلَى الَّذِينَ يَتَوَلَّوْنَهُ وَالَّذِينَ هُمْ بِهِ مُشْرِكُونَ﴾

[النحل: ١٠٠].

﴿مَن تَوَلَّاهُ فَأَنَّهُ يُضِلُّهُ﴾ [الحجّ: ٤].

وَاذْكُرْ عَهْدَ اللَّهِ عَلَيْكَ وَمِيثَاقَهُ فِي وَحْيِهِ وَتَنْزِيلِهِ، وَانْظُرْ كَيْفَ تَقْرَأُ كَلَامَهُ وَكِتَابَهُ فَرَتِّلْ وَتَدَبَّرْ، وَقِفْ عِنْدَ وَعْدِهِ وَوَعِيدِهِ وَأَمْثَالِهِ وَمَوَاعِظِهِ وَأَمْرِهِ وَنَهْيِهِ وَمُحْكَمِهِ وَمُتَشَابِهِهِ،

Furthermore, I fear that your careless attempt to implement its rulings may be regarded as a complete disregard for them.

“So what message after this ⌜Quran⌝ would they believe in?”[30]

[30] Al Mursalāt: 50

وَإِنِّي لأَخْشَى أَنْ تَكُونَ إِقَامَتُكَ حُدُودَهُ غَفْلَةً مِنْ تَضْيِيعِكَ حُدُودَهَ. قَالَ اللَّهُ عَزَّ وَجَلَّ: ﴿**فَبِأَيِّ حَدِيثٍ بَعْدَهُ يُؤْمِنُونَ**﴾ [المرسلات: ٥٠].

16
BOWING

Bow in *rukūʿ* with reverence, your heart humbled before Allāh ﷻ and your limbs submissive to His greatness. Perfect your bowing and cast away any trace of arrogance or self-importance in your obedience to His command. For you cannot fulfil His obligations except with His aid, nor can you reach the abode of His pleasure except through His mercy and grace. You can only abstain from disobedience to Allāh ﷻ through His protection, and you can only be saved from His punishment through His forgiveness. The Messenger of Allāh ﷺ said: "No one will enter Paradise by their deeds alone." They asked, "Not even you, O Messenger of Allāh ﷻ?" He replied, "Not even me, unless Allāh ﷻ envelops me in His mercy."[31]

[31] Agreed upon

بَابُ الرُّكُوعِ

وَارْكَعْ رُكُوعَ خَاشِعٍ لِلَّهِ بِقَلْبِكَ خَاضِعًا بِجَوَارِحِهِ، وَاسْتَوْفِ رُكُوعَكَ، وَانْحَطَّ عَنْ هِمَّتِكَ فِي القِيَامِ بِأَمْرِهِ، فَإِنَّكَ لَا تَقْدِرُ عَلَى أَدَاءِ فَرْضِهِ إِلا بِعَوْنِهِ، وَلَا تَبْلُغُ دَارَ رِضْوَانِهِ إِلا بِرَحْمَتِهِ، وَلَا تَسْتَطِيعُ الامْتِنَاعَ مِنْ مَعْصِيَتِهِ إِلا بِعِصْمَتِهِ، وَلَا تَنْجُو مِنْ عَذَابِهِ إِلا بِعَفْوِهِ. قَالَ رَسُولُ اللَّهِ ﷺ: «لَنْ يَدْخُلَ الجَنَّةَ أَحَدٌ بِعَمَلِهِ». قَالُوا: وَلَا أَنْتَ يَا رَسُولَ اللَّهِ؟ قَالَ: «وَلَا أَنَا إِلا أَنْ يَتَغَمَّدَنِي اللَّهُ بِرَحْمَتِهِ».

17
PROSTRATION

Prostrate to Allāh ﷻ as a humble servant, knowing that you were created from dust that is walked upon by all of creation and that your origin is a mere disdainful drop. Reflect upon your essence, formed from water and clay, and let this reflection increase your humility. Say to yourself: "Woe unto me! Why have you raised your head from your prostration? How have you not died in front of His presence when He has made the prostration the means of closeness to Him?" He ﷻ says:

"And prostrate and draw near [to Allāh]."[32]

Thus, the one who draws closer to Allāh ﷻ will inevitably distance themselves from all else. Reflect deeply on the state of prostration when reading Allāh's ﷻ words:

---

[32] Al 'Alaq: 19

بَابُ السُّجُودِ

وَاسْجُدْ لِلَّهِ سُجُودَ عَبْدٍ مُتَوَاضِعٍ عَلِمَ أَنَّهُ خُلِقَ مِنْ تُرَابٍ يَطَؤُهُ جَمِيعُ الخَلْقِ، وَأَنَّهُ رُكِّبَ مِنْ نُطْفَةٍ يَسْتَقْذِرُهَا كُلُّ أَحَدٍ. فَإِذَا فَكَّرَ فِي أَصْلِهِ وَتَأَمَّلَ تَرْكِيبَ جَوْهَرِهِ مِنْ مَاءٍ وَطِينٍ ازْدَادَ لِلَّهِ تَوَاضُعًا وَيَقُولُ فِي نَفْسِهِ: وَيْلَكَ لَمْ رَفَعْتَ رَأْسَكَ مِنْ سُجُودِكَ لِمَ لَمْ تَمُتْ وَقَدْ جَعَلَ اللَّهُ السُّجُودَ سَبَبَ الْقُرْبِ إِلَيْهِ؟ فَقَالَ تَعَالَى: ﴿**وَاسْجُدْ وَاقْتَرِبْ**﴾ [العلق: ١٩].

فَمَنْ اقْتَرَبَ مِنْهُ بَعُدَ مِنْ كُلِّ شَيْءٍ سِوَاهُ. وَاحْفَظْ صِفَةَ سُجُودِكَ فِي هَذِهِ الآيَةِ:

"From the earth We created you, and into it We will return you, and from it We will bring you back again."[33]

Seek help from Allāh ﷻ in all matters, for none can succeed except with His aid.

It is also reported from the Prophet ﷺ that Allāh ﷻ, has said: "I do not look into the heart of a servant and find within it a love for actions done in obedience to Me, except that I take over guiding and managing that servant."[34]

---

[33] Ṭahā: 55

[34] *Al Mutaḥābbīn fillāh*, Ibn Qudāmah al Maqdisi no.54 (*Dār al Ṭibā'*, Damascus)

﴿ مِنْهَا خَلَقْنَاكُمْ وَفِيهَا نُعِيدُكُمْ وَمِنْهَا نُخْرِجُكُمْ تَارَةً أُخْرَىٰ ﴾ [طه: ٥٥]، وَاسْتَعِنْ بِاللَّهِ عنْ غَيْرِهِ فإنّه رُوِيَ عَنْ النَّبِيِّ ﷺ أَنَّهُ قَالَ: "قَالَ اللَّهُ تبَارَكَ وَتَعَالَى: **لا أَطَّلعُ على قَلْبِ عبْدٍ فأَعْلَمُ منْهُ حُبَّ الْعَمَلِ بِطَاعَتِي إلا توَلَّيْتُ تقْوِيمَهُ وَسِيَاسَتَهُ**".

18
THE TESTIMONY OF FAITH

The *tashahhud* entails praising (*thanā'*) Allāh ﷻ, giving thanks to Him and seeking an increase in His favour and the continuation of His grace. Exit from your reliance on your own claims of righteousness and adopt the stance of a humble servant in both your words and actions. Be as a servant addressing his master, for He has created you as a servant and commanded you to remain as such.

Allāh ﷻ, has said,

"When God and His Messenger have decided on a matter that concerns them, it is not fitting for any believing man or woman to claim freedom of choice in that matter: whoever disobeys God and His Messenger is far astray."[35]

---

[35] Al Aḥzāb: 36

بَابُ التَّشَهُّدِ

وَالتَّشَهُّدُ ثَنَاءٌ، وَشُكْرٌ لَهُ، وَتَعَرُّضٌ لِمَزِيدِ فَضْلِهِ، وَدَوَامِ كَرَامَتِهِ، فَاخْرُجْ عَنْ دَعْوَاكَ، وَكُنْ لَهُ عَبْدًا بِفِعْلِكَ كَمَا أَنْتَ عَبْدٌ لَهُ بِقَوْلِكَ، فَإِنَّهُ خَلَقَكَ عَبْدًا وَأَمَرَكَ أَنْ تَكُونَ لَهُ عَبْدًا كَمَا خَلَقَكَ. ﴿**وَمَا كَانَ لِمُؤْمِنٍ وَلَا مُؤْمِنَةٍ إِذَا قَضَى اللَّهُ وَرَسُولُهُ أَمْرًا أَنْ يَكُونَ لَهُمُ الْخِيَرَةُ مِنْ أَمْرِهِمْ**﴾ [الأحزاب: ٣٦].

And He says,

"Your Lord creates what He pleases and chooses those He will- they have no choice."[36]

Thus, embody servitude with complete surrender to His wisdom. Engage in acts of worship with a heart content in submission to His command and His decree. Send salutations on His beloved ﷺ after praising Him, for He has made attaining His love contingent upon loving His beloved. Moreover, obedience to Him is contingent upon obeying His beloved. Allāh ﷻ says,

"Say, 'If you love God, follow me, and God will love you and forgive you your sins; God is most forgiving, most merciful."[37]

And He ﷻ said,

"Whoever obeys the Messenger has obeyed Allāh."[38]

---

[36] Al Qaṣaṣ: 688

[37] Āl ʿImrān: 31

[38] Al Nisā ʾ: 80

﴿ وَرَبُّكَ يَخْلُقُ مَا يَشَاءُ وَيَخْتَارُ ﴾ [القصص : ٦٨].

فَاسْتَعْمِلِ الْعُبُودِيَّةَ فِي الرِّضَا بِحِكْمَتِه، وَاسْتَعْمِلِ الْعِبَادَةَ فِي النزُول تَحْتَ أَمْرِه، وَصَلِّ عَلَى حَبِيبِه عَقْبَ الثَّنَاءِ عَلَيْه، فَإِنَّهُ وَصل مَحبّتَه بِمَحَبَّتِه وَطَاعَتَهُ بِطاعَتِه وَمُتَابَعَتَهُ بِمُتابعَتِه، فَقَالَ تَعَالَى : ﴿ قُلْ إِنْ كُنْتُمْ تُحِبُّونَ اللَّهَ فَاتَّبِعُونِي يُحْبِبْكُمُ اللَّهُ ﴾ [آل عمران : ٣١]. وَقَالَ : ﴿ مَنْ يُطِعِ الرَّسُولَ فَقَدْ أَطَاعَ اللَّهَ ﴾ [النساء : ٨٠].

And He ﷻ said,

"Those who pledge loyalty to you [Prophet] are actually pledging loyalty to God Himself..."[39]

Know that He ﷻ commanded His messenger to seek forgiveness for you,

"So [Prophet], bear in mind that there is no god but God, and ask forgiveness for your sins and for the sins of believing men and women."[40]

He ﷻ has also commanded you to send salutations upon him,

"Verily, God and His angels bless the Prophet: [hence,] O you who have attained to faith, bless him and give yourselves up [to his guidance] in utter self-surrender"[41]

The Messenger of Allah ﷺ said,

"Whoever sends blessings upon me once, Allah will bless them tenfold."[42]

---

[39] Al Fatḥ: 10

[40] Muḥammad: 19

[41] Al Aḥzāb: 56

[42] Muslim: 408

وقال ﴿ **إِنَّ الَّذِينَ يُبَايِعُونَكَ إِنَّمَا يُبَايِعُونَ اللَّهَ** ﴾ [الفتح : ١٠].

وَأَمَرَ رَسُولَهُ بِالاسْتِغْفَارِ لَكَ، فَقَالَ تَعَالَى : ﴿ **فَاعْلَمْ أَنَّهُ لَا إِلَهَ إِلَّا اللَّهُ وَاسْتَغْفِرْ لِذَنْبِكَ وَلِلْمُؤْمِنِينَ وَالْمُؤْمِنَاتِ** ﴾ [محمد : ١٩].

وَأَمَرَكَ بِالصَّلاةِ عَلَيْهِ، فَقَالَ تَعَالَى : ﴿ **إِنَّ اللَّهَ وَمَلَائِكَتَهُ يُصَلُّونَ عَلَى النَّبِيِّ يَا أَيُّهَا الَّذِينَ آمَنُوا صَلُّوا عَلَيْهِ وَسَلِّمُوا تَسْلِيمًا** ﴾ [الأحزاب : ٥٦]. وَقَالَ رَسُولُ اللَّهِ ﷺ : "مَنْ صَلَّى عَلَيَّ وَاحِدَةً صَلَّى اللَّهُ عَلَيْهِ بِهَا عَشْرًا."

He ﷻ treated His servant ﷺ with generosity and grace, as He ﷻ says,

"And [have We not] raised thee high in dignity"[43]

Then He commanded others to be just with him ﷺ in their dealings, as He says ﷻ,

"And when the prayer is ended, disperse freely on earth and seek to obtain [something] of God's bounty..."[44]

And He ﷻ said to him ﷺ,

"So once you have fulfilled ⸢your duty⸣, strive ⸢in devotion⸣, turning to your Lord ⸢alone⸣ with hope."[45]

---

[43] Al Sharḥ: 4

[44] Al Jumu ʿah: 10

[45] Al Sharḥ: 7-8

وَعَامَلَهُ بِالْفَضْلِ، فَقَالَ تَعَالَى: ﴿**وَرَفَعْنَا لَكَ ذِكْرَكَ**﴾ [الشرح: ٤].

ثُمَّ أَمَرَكَ بِمُعَامَلَتِهِ بِالْعَدْلِ، فَقَالَ لِغَيْرِهِ: ﴿**فَإِذَا قُضِيَتِ الصَّلَاةُ فَانْتَشِرُوا فِي الْأَرْضِ**﴾ [الجمعة: ١٠].

وَقَالَ لَهُ: ﴿**فَإِذَا فَرَغْتَ فَانْصَبْ ٧ وَإِلَى رَبِّكَ فَارْغَبْ**﴾ [الشرح: ٧-٨].

19
THE END OF THE PRAYER (*SALĀM*)

Al-Salām is one of the names of Allāh ﷻ, which He has entrusted to His creation so they may embody its meaning in their dealings and interactions with one another. If you desire peace, then let peace emanate from you to your companion, and show mercy to those who show no mercy to themselves. For indeed, creation is perpetually enveloped in trials and challenges; one is either tested with the gift of blessings to reveal their gratitude or burdened with hardship to demonstrate the depth of their patience. Allāh ﷻ, says,

" [The nature of] man is that, when his Lord tries him through honour and blessings, he says, 'My Lord has honoured me,' but when He tries him through the restriction of his provision, he says, 'My Lord has humiliated me.'"[46]

[46] Al Fajr: 15-16

بَابُ السَّلامِ

السَّلامُ اسْمٌ مِنْ أَسْمَاءِ اللَّهِ تَعَالَى أَوْدَعَهُ خَلْقَهُ لِيَسْتَعْمِلُوا مَعْنَاهُ فِي مُعَامَلَتِهِ وَمُعَاشَرَةِ خَلْقِهِ. فَإِذَا أَرَدْتَ السَّلامَةَ فَلْيَسْلَمْ مِنْكَ صَدِيقُكَ، وَارْحَمْ مَنْ لا يَرْحَمُ نَفْسَهُ، فَإِنَّ الخَلْقَ بَيْنَ فِتَنٍ وَمِحَنٍ، إِمَّا مُبْتَلًى بِالنِّعْمَةِ لِيُظْهِرَ شُكْرَهُ، وَإِمَّا مُبْتَلًى بِالشِّدَّةِ لِيُظْهِرَ صَبْرَهُ.

قَالَ اللَّهُ تَعَالَى:

﴿ فَأَمَّا الْإِنْسَانُ إِذَا مَا ابْتَلَاهُ رَبُّهُ فَأَكْرَمَهُ وَنَعَّمَهُ فَيَقُولُ رَبِّي أَكْرَمَنِ ﴿١٥﴾ وَأَمَّا إِذَا مَا ابْتَلَاهُ فَقَدَرَ عَلَيْهِ رِزْقَهُ فَيَقُولُ رَبِّي أَهَانَنِ ﴿١٦﴾ كَلَّا ﴾ [الفجر: ﴿١٥﴾-﴿١٧﴾].

True honour lies in obedience to Allāh ﷻ, whilst humiliation resides in disobedience to Him. Whoever is led by their desires will ultimately be degraded by Allāh ﷻ.

فَالْكَرَامَةُ فِي طَاعَتِهِ، وَالمَهَانَةُ فِي مَعْصِيَتِهِ، وَمَنْ رَكِبَ الْهَوَى أَهَانَهُ اللّٰهُ.

20
SUPPLICATION

Observe the etiquettes of supplication, and consider to whom you are calling, how you are calling, and why you are calling and asking. Know that the act of supplication itself is an expression of servitude where your entirety seeks a response from the Truth. If you do not fulfil this specific condition of supplication do not expect a response!

Mālik ibn Dīnār (rḥ) said, "You all consider the fall of rain to be delayed, but I consider the falling of rocks to be delayed!"[47] If Allāh ﷻ had not commanded us to make supplications, it would still have been an obligation upon us to call upon Him.

---

[47] See Ibn al Jawzi, *Ṣifah al Ṣafwah*: 1/371. In another version of this report he said, "As long as it is not raining stones, we are fine!"

بَابُ الدُّعَاءِ

وَاحْفَظْ آدَابَ الدُّعَاءِ، وَانْظُرْ مَنْ تَدْعُو، وَكَيْفَ تَدْعُو، وَلِمَاذَا تَدْعُو، وَلِمَاذَا تَسْأَلُ، وَالدُّعَاءُ اسْتِجَابَةُ الْكُلِّ مِنْكَ لِلْحَقِّ، وَإِنْ لَمْ تَأْتِ بِشَرْطِ الدُّعَاءِ، فَلا تَشْتَرِطِ الإِجَابَةَ. قَالَ مَالِكُ بْنُ دِينَارٍ: أَنْتُمْ تَسْتَبْطِئُونَ الْمَطَرَ وَأَنَا أَسْتَبْطِئُ الْحَجَرَ. وَلَوْ لَمْ يَأْمُرِ اللَّهُ سُبْحَانَهُ بِالدُّعَاءِ لَوَجَبَ عَلَيْنَا أَنْ نَدْعُوَهُ

Even though He has not made an immediate response conditional, our sincerity in supplication invites His grace and favour. How, then, can one despair when Allāh ﷻ assures us of the response to our calls? He ﷻ says,

"What are you to my Lord without your supplication?"[48]

"Your Lord says, 'Call on Me and I will answer you…'"[49]

Abū Yazīd Al Bisṭāmi (rḥ) was asked about the Greatest Name of Allāh ﷻ. He replied: "Let your heart call upon Him without any distractions or attachments, and address Him with any name that comes to your mind, for all His names are great."

Yaḥyā Ibn Mu'ādh (rḥ) said, "Seek the owner of the name Himself."

The Messenger of Allah ﷺ said to Ibn Mas'ūd:

"Allāh ﷻ does not respond to a supplication from a heedless or distracted heart."[50]

---

[48] Al Furqān: 77

[49] Al Ghāfir: 60

[50] Al Tirmidhi: 3479

وَلَوْ لَمْ يُشْتَرَطْ لَنَا الإِجَابَةُ لَكُنَّا إِذَا أَخْلَصْنَا الدُّعَاءَ تَفَضَّلَ بِالإِجَابَةِ. فَكَيْفَ وَقَدْ ضَمِنَ ذَلِكَ لِمَنْ أَتَى بِشَرْطِ الدُّعَاءِ؟ قَالَ اللَّهُ تَعَالَى: ﴿**قُلْ مَا يَعْبَأُ بِكُمْ رَبِّي لَوْلَا دُعَاؤُكُمْ**﴾ [الفرقان: ٧٧].

وَقَالَ تَعَالَى: ﴿**ادْعُونِي أَسْتَجِبْ لَكُمْ**﴾ [غافر: ٦٠].

وَسُئِلَ أَبُو يَزِيدَ الْبِسْطَامِيُّ عَنْ اسْمِ اللَّهِ الأَعْظَمِ، فَقَالَ: فَرِّغْ قَلْبَكَ مِنْ غَيْرِهِ وَادْعُهُ بِأَيِّ أَسْمَائِهِ شِئْتَ. وَقَالَ يَحْيى بْنُ مُعَاذٍ: اطْلُبْ صَاحِبَ الإِسْمِ. وَقَالَ رَسُولُ اللَّهِ ﷺ: "لا يَسْتَجِيبُ اللَّهُ الدُّعَاءَ مِنْ قَلْبٍ لاهٍ".

If you are sincere in your supplication, then anticipate one of three outcomes: either Allāh ﷻ, in His wisdom, hastens to grant you what you seek, or He reserves for you something far greater in the Hereafter, or He averts from you a harm so immense that, had it befallen you, it would have brought about your ruin. Therefore, offer a sincere supplication seriously, not with the invocation of someone who seeks to give (Allāh) advice.

It has also been narrated from the Messenger of Allāh ﷺ that Allah ﷻ, says,

"Whoever is too preoccupied with My remembrance to ask of Me, I will give him more than I give those who ask."[51]

Abū Al Ḥusayn Al Warrāq said: "I once made a supplication, and He answered it. I then later forgot how much I was in need of that supplication to be answered."

Therefore, guard the right of Allāh ﷻ regarding calling upon Him and do not become preoccupied with how or when your request will be answered, for He knows best what is good for you.

---

[51] *Shu'āb al Imān*, al Bayhaqi: 572

فَإِذَا أَخْلَصْتَ فَأَبْشِرْ بِإِحْدَى ثَلاثٍ: إِمَّا أَنْ يَجْعَلَ لَكَ مَا سَأَلْتَ، وَإِمَّا أَنْ يَدَّخِرَ لَكَ مَا هُوَ أَعْظَمُ مِنْهُ، وَإِمَّا أَنْ يَصْرِفَ عَنْكَ مِنَ الْبَلاءِ مَا لَوْ صَبَّهُ عَلَيْكَ لِهَلَكْتَ. وَادْعُ دُعَاءَ مُسْتَجْدٍ لا دُعَاءَ مُشِيرٍ.

وَرُوِيَ عَنْ رَسُولِ اللَّهِ ﷺ أَنَّهُ قَالَ: "قَالَ اللَّهُ تَبَارَكَ وَتَعَالَى: مَنْ شَغَلَهُ ذِكْرِي عَنْ مَسْأَلَتِي أَعْطَيْتُهُ أَفْضَلَ مَا أُعْطِيَ السَّائِلِينَ".

وَقَالَ أَبُو الحَسَنِ الْوَرَّاقُ: دَعَوْتُ اللَّهَ تَعَالَى مَرَّةً فَاسْتَجَابَ دُعَائِي، فَنَسِيتُ الحَاجَةَ. فَاحْفَظْ حَقَّ اللَّهِ عَزَّ وَجَلَّ عَلَيْكَ فِي الدُّعَاءِ، وَلا تَشْتَغِلْ بِحَظِّكَ، فَإِنَّهُ أَعْلَمُ بِمَصْلَحَتِكَ.

21
FASTING

When you fast, let your fasting go beyond abstaining from food and drink—restrain your soul from its desires and passions. For fasting is the annihilation of the ego, and within it lies the purification of the heart, the refinement of the limbs, an awakening to the needs of the poor, and a turning toward Allāh ﷻ in gratitude and supplication. It is a means to thank Allāh ﷻ for His countless blessings and to seek relief from the burden of accountability.

Know that Allāh's ﷻ favour in enabling you to fast is far greater than the gratitude you show for it. Whoever fasts should do so sincerely without seeking compensation, for fasting is a deed performed for Allāh ﷻ alone.

بَابُ الصَّوْمِ

فَإِذَا صُمْتَ فَانْوِ بِصَوْمِكَ كَفَّ النَّفْسِ عَنِ الشَّهَوَاتِ، فَإِنَّ الصَّوْمَ فَنَاءُ مُرَادِ النَّفْسِ، وَفِيهِ صَفَاءُ الْقَلْبِ وَضَمَارَةُ الجَوَارِحِ، وَالتَّنْبِيهُ عَلَى الإِحْسَانِ إِلَى الْفُقَرَاءِ، وَالالتِجَاءُ إِلَى اللَّهِ وَالشُّكْرُ عَلَى مَا تَفَضَّلَ بِهِ مِنَ النِّعَمِ، وَتَخْفِيفُ الحِسَابِ. وَمِنَّةُ اللَّهِ فِي تَوْفِيقِكَ لِلصَّوْمِ أَعْظَمُ مِنْ أَنْ تَقُومَ بِشُكْرِهَا، وَمِنْ صَوْمُكَ أَنْ لا تَطْلُبَ مِنْهُ عِوَضًا.

22
ZAKĀH

For every part of you, there is a form of *zakāh* that is due to Allāh ﷻ. The *zakāh* of the heart is to reflect upon His greatness, wisdom, power, proofs, blessings, and mercy. The *zakāh* of the eyes is to look with consideration and insight, to restrain them from desires. The *zakāh* of the ears is to listen to what leads to your salvation. The *zakāh* of the tongue is to speak only that which brings you nearer to Him. The *zakāh* of the hand is to refrain from harm and to extend it toward goodness. The *zakāh* of the feet is to strive toward that which brings about the rectification of your heart and the safety of your religion.

بَابُ الزَّكَاةِ

وَعَنْ كُلِّ جُزْءٍ مِنْ أَجْزَائِكَ زَكَاةٌ وَاجِبَةٌ لِلَّه، فَزَكَاةُ الْقَلْبِ: التَّفَكُّرُ فِي عَظَمَتِهِ وَحِكْمَتِهِ وَقُدْرَتِهِ وَحُجَّتِهِ وَنِعْمَتِهِ وَرَحْمَتِهِ. وَزَكَاةُ الْعَيْنِ: النَّظَرُ بِالْعِبْرَةِ وَالْغَضُّ عَنِ الشَّهْوَةِ. وَزَكَاةُ الأُذُنِ: الاسْتِمَاعُ إِلَى مَا فِيهِ نَجَاتُكَ. وَزَكَاةُ اللِّسَانِ: النُّطْقُ بِمَا يُقَرِّبُكَ إِلَيْهِ. وَزَكَاةُ الْيَدِ: الْقَبْضُ عَنِ الشَّرِّ وَالْبَسْطُ إِلَى الخَيْرِ. وَزَكَاةُ الرِّجْلِ: السَّعْيُ إِلَى مَا فِيهِ صَلاحُ قَلْبِكَ وَسَلامَةُ دِينِكَ.

23
THE PILGRIMAGE

When someone intends to perform Ḥajj, let them resolve their intention with a heart filled with fear of rejection and let them prepare for this sacred journey as one who does not expect to return. They should select the best companions, and free themselves from their lower selves at the time of *iḥrām* and wash away their sins. They should also adorn themselves with garments of truth and loyalty.

Let their *talbiyah* be in response to His call. Let them make ihram with a heart that has renounced all else but Him, and sanctify themselves from anything that displeases Allāh ﷻ. As they circumambulate the Kaʿbah, they should do so with their hearts seeing themselves standing before Allāh's ﷻ Throne, turning their entire being toward His honour and greatness. When they perform *saʿī* (walking between Ṣafā and Marwā), let their outward steps reflect the inward journey of purifying their soul, removing their desires, and freeing themselves from the bondage of sin.

بَابُ الحَجِّ

وَالْمُرِيدُ إِذَا حَجَّ يَعْقِدُ النِّيَّةَ خَوْفَ الرَّدِّ، وَاسْتَعَدَّ اسْتِعْدَادَ مَنْ لا يَرْجُو الإِيَابَ، وَأَحْسَنَ الصُّحْبَةَ، وَتَجَرَّدَ عِنْدَ الإِحْرَامِ عَنْ نَفْسِهِ، وَاغْتَسَلَ مِنْ ذَنْبِهِ، وَلَبِسَ ثَوْبُ الصِّدْقِ وَالْوَفَاءِ، وَلَبَّى مُوَافَقَةً لِلْحَقِّ فِي إِجَابَةِ دَعْوَتِهِ، وَأَحْرَمَ فِي الحَرَمِ مِنْ كُلِّ شَيْءٍ يُبْعِدُهُ عَنْ اللَّهِ تَعَالَى، وَطَافَ بِقَلْبِهِ حَوْلَ كُرْسِيِّ كَرَامَتِهِ، وَصَفَّى ظَاهِرَهُ وَبَاطِنَهُ عِنْدَ الْوُقُوفِ عَلَى الصَّفَا، وَهَرْوَلَ هَرَباً مِنْ هَوَاهُ، وَلَمْ يَتَمَنَّ عَلَى اللَّهِ تَعَالَى مَا لا يَحِلُّ لَهُ

When they stand at ʿArafah, let them stand with full recognition of their sins and let them draw closer to Him at Muzdalifah. Let them cast their stones at the *Jamarāt* with the intention of casting away their own base desires. As they sacrifice, let them sacrifice their ego and as they shave, let them shave away their sins.

As they conclude their rites and visit the sacred house, let them venerate its owner, and let them touch the black stone in contentment with His decrees. And when they bid farewell, let them bid farewell to all else besides Allāh ﷻ.

وَاعْتَرَفَ بِخَطَئِهِ بِعَرَفَةَ، وَتَقَرَّبَ إِلَى اللَّهِ بِمُزْدَلِفَةَ، وَرَمَى الشَّهَوَاتِ عِنْدَ رَمْيِ الجِمَارَاتِ، وَذَبَحَ هَوَاهُ وَحَلَقَ الذُّنُوبَ، وَزَارَ الْبَيْتَ مُعَظِّماً صَاحِبَهُ، وَاسْتَلَمَ الحَجَرَ رِضَاءً بِقَضَائِهِ، وَوَدَّعَ مَا دُونَ اللَّهِ فِي طَوَافِ الْوَدَاعِ.

24
SECURITY OF FAITH

Seek security of faith (*salāmah*). If only those who truly sought it could find it! What, then, can be said of those who recklessly expose themselves to tribulation?

In this age, such security has become exceedingly rare and is found only in anonymity (*khumūl*). If it cannot be attained through anonymity, then it may be found in seclusion (*ʿuzlah*). However, know that seclusion is not the same as anonymity. If one cannot find it in seclusion, then it may be sought in silence, although silence is not equivalent to seclusion. And if it cannot be found in silence, then it may be attained in beneficial speech that causes no harm, although it is not the same as silence.

If you seek security, refrain from disputes and arguments, and avoid competition and contention over worldly matters.

بَابُ السَّلامَةِ

وَاطْلُبِ السَّلامَةَ فَلَيْتَ مَنْ طَلَبَهَا وَجَدَهَا فَكَيْفَ لِمَنْ تَعَرَّضَ لِلْبَلاءِ، وَالسَّلامَةُ قَدْ عَزَّتْ فِي هَذَا الزَّمَانِ وَهِيَ فِي الخمول، فَإِنْ لَمْ تَكُنْ فِي الخمول، فَالْعُزْلَةُ وَلَيْسَتْ كَالخمول، فَإِنْ لَمْ تَكُنْ عُزْلة فالصمت وليس كالعُزْلَة فإنْ لم تَكُن فِي صَمْتٍ فَالْكَلامُ بِمَا يَنْفَعُ وَلا يَضُرُّ وَلَيْسَ كَالْصَّمْتِ. وَإِنْ أَرَدْتَ السَّلامَةَ فَلا تُنَازِعْ الأَضْدَادَ وَلا تُنَافِسِ الأَشْكَالَ.

When someone says, "I," respond with, "you" and when they say, "for me," reply with, "for you." True safety is found in abandoning blameworthy customs and practices, which is achieved by erasing individual desires (*irādah*) and relinquishing any claims to knowing Allah's plans. Entrust all matters to Him, for He alone manages the affairs of His creation.

Allāh ﷻ, says,

"Is Allah not sufficient for His servant?"[52]

And He ﷻ says,

"He conducts every affair from the heavens to the earth..."[53]

---

[52] Al Zumar: 36

[53] Al Sajdah: 5

كُلُّ مَنْ قَالَ أَنَا فَقُلْ أَنْتَ، وَكُلُّ مَنْ قَالَ لِي فَقُلْ لَكَ. وَالسَّلامَةُ فِي زَوَالِ الْعرْفِ، وزَوَالُ الْعرْفِ فِي فَقْدِ الإِرَادَةِ، وَفَقْدُ الإِرَادَةِ فِي تَرْكِ دَعْوَى الْعِلْمِ فِيمَا اسْتَأْثَرَ اللَّهُ بِهِ مِنْ تَدْبِيرِ أَمْرِكَ. قَالَ اللَّهُ تَعَالَى: ﴿أَلَيْسَ اللهُ بِكَافٍ عَبْدَهُ﴾ [الزمر: ٣٦].

وَقَالَ: ﴿يُدَبِّرُ الْأَمْرَ مِنَ السَّمَاءِ إِلَى الْأَرْضِ﴾ [السجدة: ٥].

25
SECLUSION

The one who adopts seclusion must equip themselves with ten things:

1. Knowledge of truth and falsehood.
2. Detachment from worldly desires and enduring hardships.
3. Taking advantage of solitude and finding safety in it.
4. Reflecting on consequences and outcomes.
5. Recognising the superiority of others over oneself.
6. Distancing others from the evil of oneself.
7. Not ceasing in goodness, for idleness can be a trial.
8. Not admiring one's state.

بَابُ الْعُزْلَة

صَاحِبُ الْعُزْلَةِ يَحْتَاجُ إِلَى عَشَرَةِ أَشْيَاءَ:

- عِلْمُ الحَقِّ وَالْبَاطِلِ،
- وَالزُّهْدُ وَاخْتِيَارُ الشِّدَّةِ،
- وَاغْتِنَامُ الخَلْوَةِ وَالسَّلامَةِ،
- وَالنَّظَرُ فِي الْعَوَاقِبِ،
- وَأَنْ يَرَى غَيْرَهُ أَفْضَلَ مِنْهُ،
- وَيَعْزِلَ عَنْ النَّاسِ شَرَّهُ،
- وَلا يَفْتُرَ عَنِ الْعَمَلِ، فَإِنَّ الْفَرَاغَ بَلاءٌ،
- وَلا يَعْجَب بِمَا هُوَ فِيهِ

9. Simplifying one's home by removing excess possessions. For the people of *Irādah* (seeking the divine), excess is defined as having more than a day's worth of supplies and for the people of *Maʿrifah* (gnosis) it is to have more than your needs in the present.
10. The one in seclusion must cut off what severs them from Allāh ﷻ.

The Prophet ﷺ said to Hudhayfah ibn Al Yamān

"Stay rooted in the confines of your home."[54]

It was said by 'Isā the son of Maryam:

"Control your tongue, let your home be enough for you, and regard yourself as a harmful predator or a consuming fire. Indeed, people were once like leaves without thorns, offering shade and ease, but now they have become thorns without leaves, causing harm without benefit. They used to be like medicine that healed the ailments of others, but now they have become the very diseases themselves, incurable and harmful."

---

[54] Abū Dāwūd (4262), although narrated by Abū Mūsā al Ash'ari and mentioned in the plural: "كُونُوا أَحْلَاسَ بُيُوتِكُمْ"

- وَيَخْلو بَيْتَهُ مِنَ الْفُضُولِ، وَالْفُضُولُ مَا فَضَلَ عَنْ يَوْمِكَ لأَهْلِ الإِرَادَةِ، وَمَا فَضَلَ عَنْ وَقْتِكَ لأَهْلِ المَعْرِفَةِ،
- وَيَقْطَعُ مَا يَقْطَعُهُ عَنْ اللَّهِ تَعَالَى.

قَالَ رَسُولُ اللَّهِ ﷺ لِحُذَيْفَةَ بْنِ الْيَمَانِ: "كُنْ حِلْسَ بَيْتِكَ."

وَقَالَ عِيسَى ابْنُ مَرْيَمَ عَلَيْهِ السَّلامُ: "أَمْلِكْ لِسَانَكَ، وَالْزَمْ بَيْتَكَ، وَأَنْزِلْ نَفْسَكَ مَنْزِلَةَ السَّبْعِ الضَّارِي وَالنَّارِ الْمُحْرِقَةِ. وَقَدْ كَانَ النَّاسُ وَرَقًا بِلا شَوْكٍ فَصَارُوا شَوْكًا بِلا وَرَقٍ، وَكَانُوا أَدْوَاءً يُسْتَشْفَى بِهِمْ فَصَارُوا دَاءً لا دَوَاءَ لَهُ."

It was said to Dāwūd Al-Ṭā'i:

"Why do you not mingle with people?"

He replied:

"How can I mix with people who seek out my faults? They are either an elderly man unaware of the truth[55] or a young person who shows no respect. Whoever finds solace in Allāh ﷻ will inevitably feel estranged from others."

Fuḍayl ibn 'Iyāḍ said:

"If you can live in a place where no one knows you, then do so."

Abū Sulaymān al Dārāni said:

"My desire from this world is to don the simple garments of a shepherd and reside in a village where no one knows me, with no provision for either lunch or dinner."

---

[55] In both printed editions it states الخلق . I have chosen to translate it according to the University of King Saud manuscript (see p.112) where it states: الحق as it seems more correct in meaning. However, I could not locate this saying in any other source.

قِيلَ لِدَاوُدَ الطَّائِيِّ: "مَالَكَ لا تُخَالِطُ النَّاسَ؟" فَقَالَ: "كَيْفَ أُخَالِطُ مَنْ يَتَبَعُ عُيُوبِي كَبِيرٌ لا يَعْرِفُ الحقَّ وَصَغِيرٌ لا يُوقِّرُ مَنْ اسْتَأْنَسَ بِاللهِ اسْتَوْحَشَ مِنْ غَيْرِهِ"

وَقَالَ الْفُضَيْلُ: "إِنِ اسْتَطَعْتَ أَنْ تَكُونَ فِي مَوْضِعٍ لا تُعْرَفُ وَلا تَعْرِفُ فَافْعَلْ."

وَقَالَ سُلَيْمَانُ: "هَمِّي مِنَ الدُّنْيَا أَنْ أَلْبس عَبَاءة وَأكون بِقَرْبَةٍ ليس فِيها أحدٌ يَعرِفني ولا غذاء لي ولا عشاء."

The Messenger of Allah ﷺ said:

"There will come a time when the one who holds fast to their religion will be like someone grasping a burning coal, and their reward will be equivalent to that of fifty of you."[56]

In seclusion there is:

- The preservation of the limbs.
- Emptiness of the heart (from distractions).
- Release from the obligations of dealing with people.
- The closing of the doors to worldly concerns.
- The breaking of the Satan's weapon.
- The cultivation of both the outward and inward self.

[56] Abū Dāwūd (4341) with different wording.

وَقَالَ رَسُولُ اللَّهِ ﷺ : **"يأْتِي زمانٌ المتَمسِّك يومَئذٍ بدينه كالقَابِضِ على الجمر وله أجرُ خمْسينَ منْكم"**

وفي العُزْلَة :

- صِيَانَةُ الجَوَارِحِ،
- وَفَرَاغُ الْقَلْبِ،
- وَسُقُوطُ حُقُوقِ الخَلْقِ،
- وَإِغْلاقُ أَبْوَابِ الدُّنْيَا،
- وَكَسْرُ سِلاحِ الشَّيْطَانِ،
- وَعِمَارَةُ الظَّاهِرِ وَالْبَاطِنِ.

26
WORSHIP

Focus on fulfilling the obligatory acts, for if your obligations are safe, then what you missed will not harm you. Strive for the supererogatory (*nawāfil*) to preserve the obligatory acts, and every time you increase in worship, let it be done with gratitude and fear.

Yaḥyā Ibn Muʿādh said:

"I am amazed at someone who seeks to perform voluntary acts while neglecting an obligation. Whoever owes a debt and gives the owner of the debt the like of that which is due to him will still be required to pay the debt when the settlement is due."

Abū Bakr Al Warrāq said:

"In these times, ensure that you cultivate four qualities, each rooted in a foundational principle:

بَابُ الْعِبَادَةِ

أَقْبِلْ عَلَى أَدَاءِ الْفَرَائِضِ، فَإِنْ سَلِمَ لَكَ فَرْضُكَ فَأَنْتَ أَنْتَ، وَاطْلُبْ بِالنَّوَافِلِ حِفْظَ الْفَرَائِضِ، وَكُلَّمَا ازْدَدْتَ عِبَادَةً فَازْدَدْ شُكْرًا وَخَوْفًا.

قَالَ يَحْيَى بْنُ مُعَاذٍ: "عَجِبْتُ لِطَالِبِ فَضِيلَةٍ تَارِكِ فَرِيضَةٍ، وَمَنْ كَانَ عَلَيْهِ دَيْنٌ فَأَهْدَى إِلَى صَاحِبِ الدَّيْنِ مِثْلَ حَقِّهِ كَانَ مُطَالَبًا بِالحَقِّ إِذَا حَلَّ الأَجَلُ."

وَقَالَ أَبُو بَكْرٍ الْوَرَّاقُ: "ابْذُلْ فِي هَذَا الزَّمَانِ أَرْبَعَةً عَلَى أَرْبَعَةٍ:

1. Let voluntary acts be built upon the foundation of obligatory acts.
2. Let the outer state reflect the inner state.
3. Let outward character be grounded in the refinement of the inner self.
4. Let speech be rooted in and supported by action."

- الْفَضَائِلَ عَلَى الْفَرَائِضِ،
- وَالظَّاهِرَ عَلَى الْبَاطِنِ،
- و الخلق عَلَى النَّفْسِ،
- وَالْكَلامَ عَلَى الْفِعْلِ.

27
REFLECTION

Reflect upon the words of Allāh ﷻ,

"Was there not a period of time when man was nothing to speak of?"[57]

Contemplate your own state, recall how you have been, and take heed from what has passed of this world - has it spared anybody? For what remains of it is as fleeting as what has already departed.

The Messenger of Allāh ﷺ said,

"Nothing remains of this world except tribulations and trials."[58]

---

[57] Al Insān: 1

[58] Ibn Mājah: 4035

بَابُ التَّفَكُّرِ

تَفَكَّرْ فِي قَوْلِهِ عَزَّ وَجَلَّ: ﴿**هَلْ أَتَى عَلَى الْإِنسَانِ حِينٌ مِنَ الدَّهْرِ لَمْ يَكُنْ شَيْئًا مَذْكُورًا**﴾ [الإنسان: ١].

وَاذْكُرْ كَيْفَ أَحْوَالُكَ وَاعْتَبِرْ بِمَا مَضَى مِنَ الدُّنْيَا عَلَى مَا تَرَاهُ، هَلْ أَبْقَتْ عَلَى أَحَدٍ، وَمَا بَقِيَ مِنْهَا أَشْبَهُ بِمَا مَضَى مِنَ المَاءِ بِالمَاءِ.

وَقَدْ قَالَ رَسُولُ اللَّهِ ﷺ: "**لَمْ يَبْقَ مِنَ الدُّنْيَا إِلَّا بَلَاءٌ وَفِتْنَةٌ.**"

It is also said that Prophet Nūḥ was asked:

"How did you find this world after having lived the longest among the prophets?" He replied:

"It is like entering a house with two doors. I entered through one door, and I left through the other."

Reflection is the foundation of all goodness, for it is a mirror that reveals good and evil, revealing the reality of your deeds.

Praise be to Allah for His assistance and enabling grace, and all thanks are due to Him alone.

وَقيلَ لِنُوحٍ عَلَيْهِ السَّلامُ: "**كَيْفَ وَجَدْتَ الدُّنْيا بِأَطْوَلِ الأَنْبِياءِ عُمْراً؟**"

قَالَ: "**كَبَيْتٍ لَهُ بابَانِ، دَخَلْتُ مِنْ أَحَدِهِمَا وَخَرَجْتُ مِن الآخَرِ.**"

وَالْفِكْرَةُ أَبُو كُلِّ خَيْرٍ، وَهِيَ مِرْآةٌ تُرِيكَ الحَسَنَاتِ وَالسَّيِّئَاتِ.

تَمَّ بِحَمْدِ اللَّهِ وَعَوْنِهِ وَحُسْنِ تَوْفِيقِهِ، وَالحَمْدُ لِلَّهِ وَحْدَهُ.

APPENDIX

Attribution of the text to Imām al Ghazāli (rḥ)

As touched upon in my introduction, the text has been published under Imām al Ghazāli's name by several publishers. The text is mentioned by Brockelmann[59] as having been in a published compilation of al Ghazāli's treatises entitled *Farā'id al-La'āli min Rasā'il al Ghazāli*, (ed. Fajr Allāh al-Kurdī), Cairo, 1343/1924, pp. 101-120, which contains *Miʿrāj al-Sālikīn, Minhāj al-ʿĀrifīn*[60] and *Rawḍah al-Tālibīn*. The treatise was then republished in Beirut in a compilation of al Ghazāli's works entitled *Majmūʿah Rasā'il al Imām al Ghazāli*. It was also published in 1968 by *Maṭbaʿah al Maʿārif* under al Ghazāli's name[61] and was also printed again by Dār al Muqaṭṭam, Cairo, 2009.

A manuscript of it can be found in Maktabah al Fātih, Istanbul under the title *Manāhij al ʿĀrifīn*, no. 2896.[62] There is also a manuscript of the text in the

[59] *Geschichte der Arabischen Litteratur*, Vol. 1, Leiden, 1943-1949, p. 745

[60] See Image: 1

[61] See image: 2

[62] Al Badawi, *Mu'allafāt al Ghazāli*, Wakālah al Maṭbūʿāt, Kuwait, 1977, p.250. According to my findings, manuscript 2896 is actually a work belonging to Sayf al Dīn al Āmidi "*Ibkār al Afkār fī Uṣūl al Dīn.*"

Maktabah Azhariyyah no.1342 although I have not yet been able to procure a copy of the manuscript.

It should be noted though that the text is not commonly known as one of Imām al Ghazāli's works, and it is not cited by many as being so (such as al Subki in his *Ṭabaqāt al Shāfiʿiyyah*). To treat this issue in more detail, the following will be discussed:

1. Those who attributed the text to al Ghazāli
2. Those who considered it to be the same as another attributed text to al Ghazāli "*Minhāj al ʿĀbidīn*"
3. Those who doubted its attribution to al Ghazāli and their reasons.

Those who attributed the text to al Ghazāli

In addition to those who published the text under al Ghazāli's name, the following researchers and academics considered the authorship to be correct:

- Dr ʿĀmir al Najjār[63]
- Carl Brockelmann
- Louis Massignon

[63] *Naẓarāt fi fikr al Ghazāli,* Dār al Ma'ārif, 1992. P.125 under the name *Manāhij al 'Ārifīn* although he considers the manuscript to be lost.

- Tāshköprüzāde Ahmed Efendi[64]

Those who considered it to be the same as another attributed text to al Ghazāli "*Minhāj al 'Ābidīn*"

The comparison of the two published texts reveals clear differences in both content and length. *Minhāj al ʿĀbidīn* is notably more well-known than the current text, with a greater number of manuscripts available. Tāshkopruzāde references *Minhāj al ʿĀrifīn* as a summary of the *Iḥyāʾ* and regards it as one of al-Ghazāli's final works. However, he does not mention *Minhāj al ʿĀbidīn*, which has led some scholars to speculate that the two titles might refer to the same work. It is possible that Tāshkopruzāde was mistaken about the title and was, in fact, referring to *Minhāj al ʿĀbidīn* rather than *Minhāj al ʿĀrifīn*. Interestingly, I have come across a manuscript titled *Minhāj al-ʿĀrifīn*, although its content appears to be an Ottoman Turkish translation of *Minhāj al ʿĀbidīn*.[65]

It is also interesting to note that Imām al Qurṭubi cites *Minhāj al ʿĀrifīn* in his exegesis although the statement that he quotes is not found in *Minhāj al ʿĀrifīn*

---

[64] See article: Some aspects of Sufism in Minhāj al 'Ārifīn of al Ghazāli, p.63, Che Zarrina Sa'ari

[65] The manuscript can be found in the University of Leipzig Cod. Turc. 58. See images 3&4 for samples.

but most likely is from *Minhāj al ʿĀbidīn.*[66]

Those who doubted its attribution to al Ghazāli and their reasons.

Miguel Asín Palacios[67] doubted the attribution of the text to Al Ghazāli due to two reasons:

1. The title of the text does not really match the contents of the text.
2. The author does not cite any of his other works within the text, which is unlike al Ghazāli who regularly cites his other works.[68]

However, as al Badawi noted, the first claim seems very far-fetched since the topics of this small treatise fall exactly in line with its title. As for the second point, whilst it is true the author does not refer to his other works, it is difficult to negate al Ghazāli's authorship of the text based on that premise. Nevertheless, al Badawi

---

[66] See: al Qurṭubi, *Al Jāmiʿ li Aḥkām al Qur'ān*, Dār al Kutub al Miṣriyyah, 1964, 7/320

[67] Miguel Asín Palacios (1871–1944) was a Spanish Arabist, orientalist, and Catholic priest renowned for his pioneering studies on the intellectual and cultural exchanges between the Islamic and Christian worlds during the Middle Ages. He is most famous for drawing connections between Islamic philosophy and mysticism and Western theological and literary traditions.

[68] See al Badawi p.249

concedes that the treatise is not widely considered to be from his established works.

In addition to the above, a further manuscript of the treatise was found in the King Saud University (no. 21808). The manuscript dates to approximately the 12th century (hijri). However, it is clear that whilst the text is identical to the treatise, it is attributed to an entirely different scholar; al Muqri' Nūr al Dīn Abū al Ḥasan ibn Yūsuf al Shāfiʿī.[69] I have not come across any other bibliographical works of al Ghazāli that has noted this.

In conclusion, determining with certainty whether this text was authored by al Ghazāli remains challenging. Nevertheless, it bears significant resemblance to his established works and ideas. Upon thorough examination, no elements were identified that deviate from his line of thought. Instead, the text aligns consistently with his philosophical outlook and approach to Islamic spirituality. Ultimately, Allāh knows best.

---

[69] See images 5&6

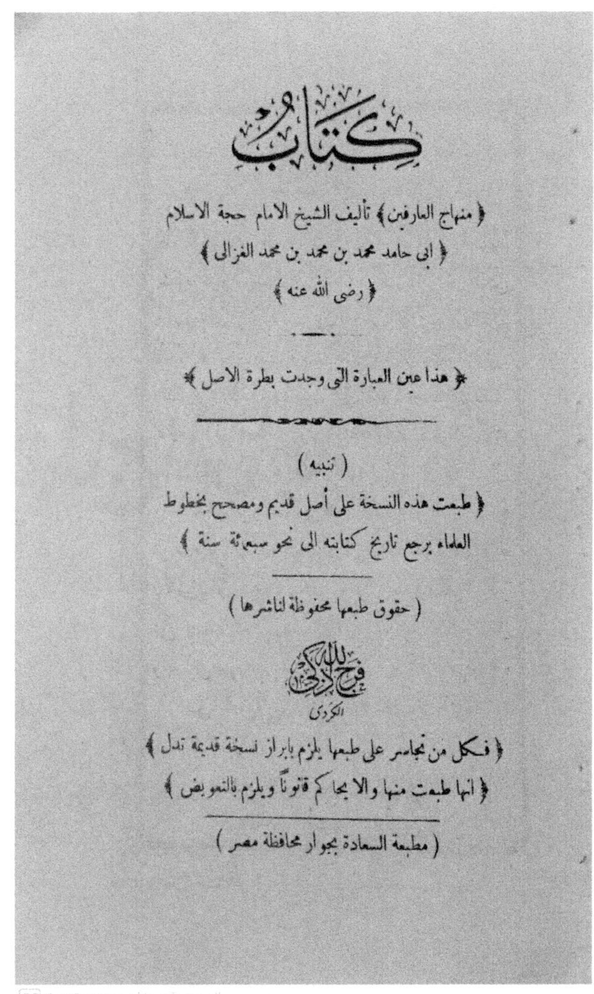

كتاب

﴿ منهاج العارفين ﴾ تأليف الشيخ الامام حجة الاسلام

﴿ ابى حامد محمد بن محمد بن محمد الغزالى ﴾

﴿ رضى الله عنه ﴾

﴿ هذا عين العبارة التى وجدت بطرة الاصل ﴾

(تنبيه)

﴿ طبعت هذه النسخة على أصل قديم ومصحح بخطوط

العلماء يرجع تاريخ كتابته الى نحو سبعمئة سنة ﴾

(حقوق طبعها محفوظة لناشرها)

فرج الله زكى

الكردى

﴿ فكل من تجاسر على طبعها يلزم بابراز نسخة قديمة تدل ﴾

﴿ انها طبعت منها والا يحاكم قانوناً ويلزم بالتعويض ﴾

(مطبعة السعادة بجوار محافظة مصر)

Image 1

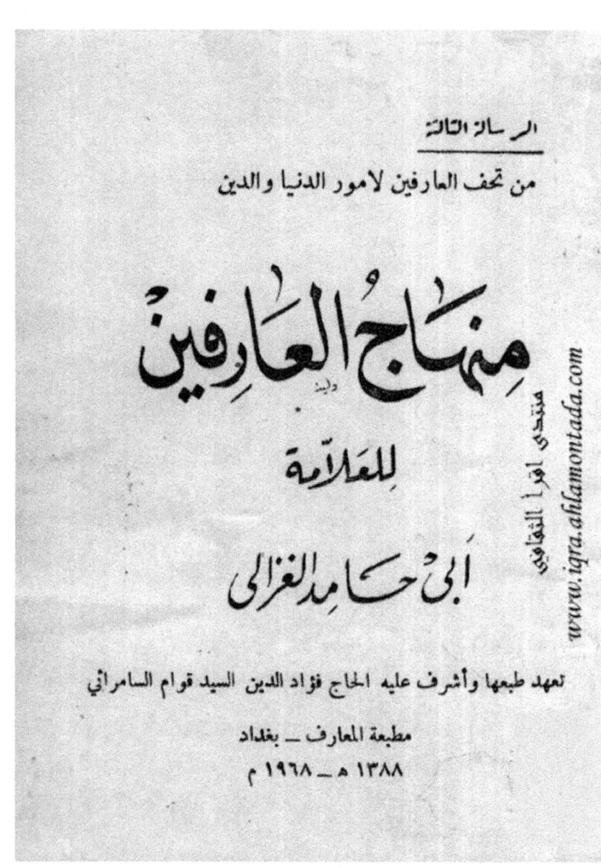

الرسالة الثالثة

من تحف العارفين لامور الدنيا والدين

منهاج العارفين

للعلامة

ابى حامد الغزالى

تعهد طبعها وأشرف عليه الحاج فؤاد الدين السيد قوام السامرائي

مطبعة المعارف ـ بغداد

١٣٨٨ هـ ـ ١٩٦٨ م

Image: 2

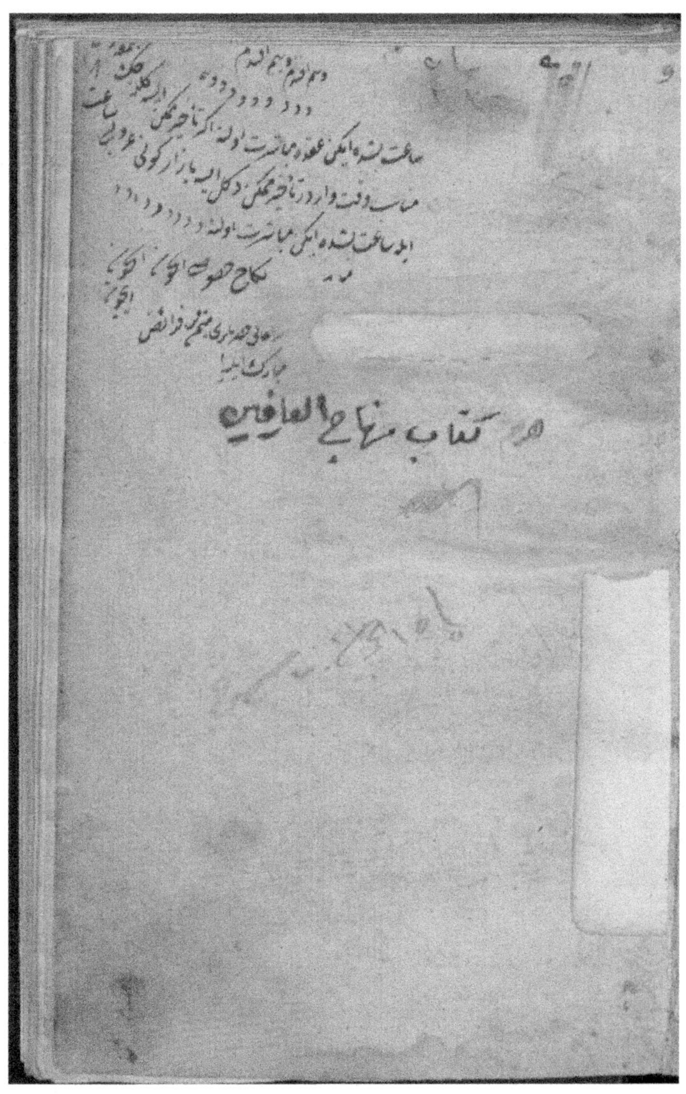

Image 3

حمد جمیل بی حد و شکر جزیل بی عد اول خالق
کونین و رازق ثقلینه که کوهر مخلوقاتک وجودی انک
جودی بحرندن بر قطره و جهانی پرتوندن بر لمعه در
و مصنوعات کائنات و نظام امور ممکنات انک بر یک
و وارلغینه دلیل قاطع و برهان ساطعدر و صلوات
بی غایات و تحیات بی نهایات اول پیشوای امت و
رهنمای ملت پادشاه تختگاه شریعت آفتاب جهانتاب
طریقت و حقیقت مرآت صفات خدا حضرت محمد
مصطفی اوزرینه اولسون که خاتم نگین نبوت
و مسند نشین مروتدر و دخی بدور بروج قرابت
و کواکب ثواقب هدایت الکرام و اصحاب عظام اوزرینه
اولسونکه بونلر اجله ممالک سیادت و ادله مسالک
سعادتدر اما بعد ای رهروان شریعت و ای سالکان

طریقت

Image 4

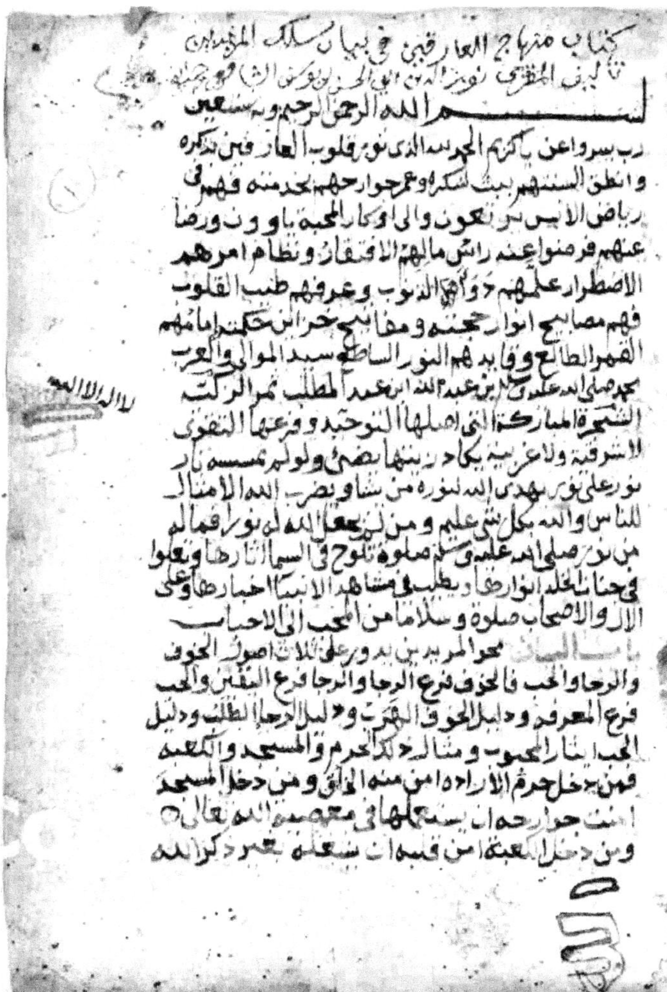

كتاب منهاج العارفين في بيان سلوك المريدين
[illegible]
بسم الله الرحمن الرحيم وبه نستعين
رب يسر واعن يا كريم الحمد لله الذي نور قلوب العارفين بذكره
وانطق السنتهم بثبت شكره وعمر جوارحهم بخدمته فهم في
رياض الانس يرتعون والى اوكار المحبة ياوون ورضا
عنهم فرضوا عنه راس مالهم الافتقار ونظام امرهم
الاضطرار علمهم دوا الذنوب وعرفهم طب القلوب
فهم مصابيح انوار حضرته ومفاتيح خزائن حكمته امامهم
القمر الطالع وقايدهم النور الساطع سيد الموالي والعرب
محمد صلى الله عليه وسلم ابن عبد الله ابن عبد المطلب ثمر البركة
الشجرة المباركة التي اصلها التوحيد وفرعها التقوى
لا شرقية ولا غربية يكاد زيتها يضيء ولو لم تمسسه نار
نور على نور يهدي الله لنوره من يشاء ويضرب الله الامثال
للناس والله بكل شيء عليم ومن لم يجعل الله له نورا فما له
من نور صلى الله عليه وسلم صلوة تلوح في السما آثارها وتعلوا
في جنان الخلد انوارها وتطيب في مشاهد الانبيا اخبارها وعلى
الال والاصحاب صلوة وسلاما من المحب الى الاحباب
[illegible] مدار المريدين يدور على ثلاث اصول الخوف
والرجا والحب فالخوف فرع العلم والرجا فرع اليقين والحب
فرع المعرفة ودليل الخوف الهرب ودليل الرجا الطلب ودليل
الحب ايثار المحبوب ومثال ذلك الحرم والمسجد والكعبة
فمن دخل حرم الارادة امن منه الاذى ومن دخل المسجد
امنت جوارحه ان يستعملها في معصية الله تعالى
ومن دخل الكعبة امن قلبه ان يشغله بغير ذكر الله

Image 5

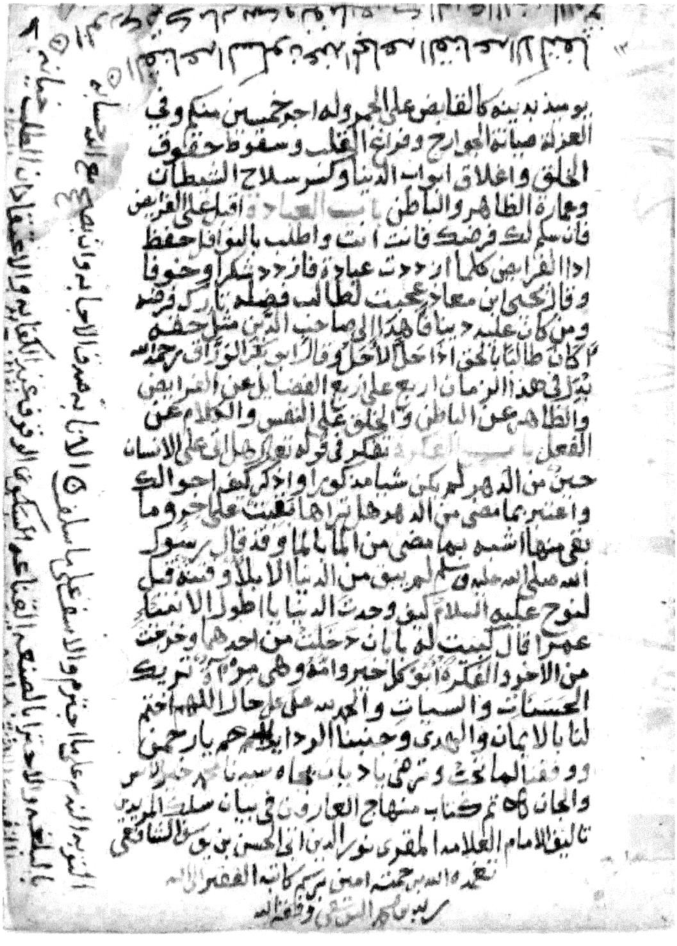

يومئذ بدينه كالقابض على الجمر وله اجر خمسين منكم وفي
العزلة صيانة الجوارح وفراغ القلب وسقوط حقوق
الخلق واغلاق ابواب الدنيا وكسر سلاح الشيطان
وعمارة الظاهر والباطن باب العبادة واقبل على الفرايض
فان سلم لك فرضك فانت انت واطلب بالنوافل حفظ
الفرايض كلما ازددت عبادة فازدد شكرا وخوفا
وقال يحيى بن معاذ عجبت لطالب فضيلة تارك فريضة
ومن كان عليه دين فاهدا الى صاحب الدين مثل حقه
كان طالبا بالحق اذا عجل الاجل وقال الربيع الوراق رحمه الله
بدل في هذا الزمان اربع على اربع الفضايل عن الفرايض
والظاهر عن الباطن والخلق على النفس والكلام عن
الفعل باب الفكرة تفكر في قوله تعالى هل اتى على الانسان
حين من الدهر لم يكن شيئا مذكورا واذكر كيف احوالك
واعتبر بما مضى من الدهر هل تراها بقيت على احد وما
بقي منها اشبه بما مضى من الماء بالماء وقد قال رسول
الله صلى الله عليه وسلم لم يبق من الدنيا الا بلاء وفتنة وقيل
لنوح عليه السلام كيف وجدت الدنيا يا اطول الانبياء
عمرا قال كبيت له بابان دخلت من احدهما وخرجت
من الاخر باب الفكرة [illegible] وهي مرآة تريك
الحسنات والسيئات والحمد لله على كل حال اللهم اختم
لنا بالايمان والهدى وحسن الرد يا ارحم الراحمين
ووفقنا للصالحات [illegible]
والجان تم كتاب منهاج العارفين في بيان سلك المريد
تاليف الامام العلامة المقري نور الدين ابي الحسن بن [illegible] الشافعي

Image 6

Bibliography

Al Badawi, ʻAbd al Raḥmān. *Mu'allafāt al Ghazāli.* Kuwait: Wakālah al Maṭbū'āt, 1977

al Ghazāli, Abū Ḥāmid. *Minhāj al ʻĀrifīn.* Bagdad: Maṭba'ah al Ma'ārif, 1986

al Ghazāli, Abū Ḥāmid. *Minhāj al ʻĀrifīn.* Cairo: Dār al Muqaṭṭam, 2010.

Tāshköprüzāde, Aḥmad ibn Muṣṭafā. *Miftāḥ al Sa'ādah wa Misbāḥ al Siyādah fī Mawḍū'āt al ʻUlūm.* Beirut: Dār al Kutub al ʻIlmiyyah.

Al ʻUthmān, ʻAbd al Karīm. *Sīrah al Ghazāli.* Damascus: Dār al Fikr.